! ! ! ! ! ! ! ! ! ! ! ! !

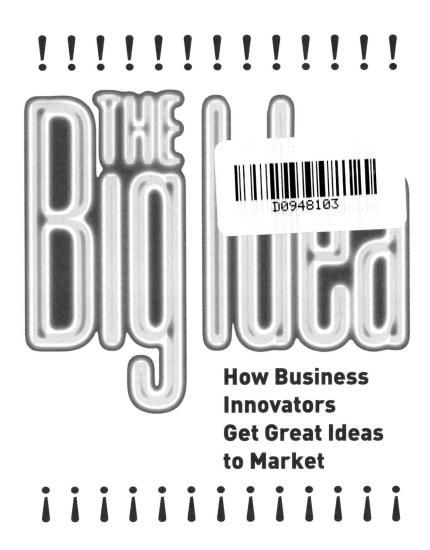

**How Business
Innovators
Get Great Ideas
to Market**

¡ ¡ ¡ ¡ ¡ ¡ ¡ ¡ ¡ ¡ ¡ ¡ ¡

Steven D. Strauss

Dearborn™
Trade Publishing
A **Kaplan Professional** Company

Dedication

To R. Buckminster Fuller

Acquisitions Editor: Mary B. Good
Senior Managing Editor: Jack Kiburz
Interior Design: Lucy Jenkins
Cover Design: design literate, inc.
Typesetting: Elizabeth Pitts

Published by Dearborn Trade Publishing, a Kaplan Professional Company

Printed in the United States of America

02 03 04 10 9 8 7 6 5 4 3 2 1

Library of Congress Cataloging-in-Publication Data

Strauss, Steven D., 1958–
   The big idea : how business innovators get great ideas to market / by Steven D. Strauss.
      p.   cm.
   Includes bibliographical references and index.
   ISBN 0-7931-4837-5 (pbk.)
   1. New products—Marketing.   I. Title.
HF5415.153 .S768   2002
658.5′75—dc21

2001004758

Dearborn Trade books are available at special quantity discounts to use for sales promotions, employee premiums, or educational purposes. Please call our Special Sales Department to order or for more information, at 800-621-9621, ext. 4307, or write Dearborn Trade Publishing, 155 N. Wacker Drive, Chicago, IL 60606-1719.

!!

Contents

6. Resistance Is Futile 149

7. Patience Is a Virtue 179

8. The Seven Great Lessons of Innovation 207

!!!

Preface

Innovation. Businesses want it. Individuals crave it. Organizations strive for it. But what does it take, really, to innovate? If you are looking for a theoretical framework and long exposition discussing the pros and cons of various business methodologies, then you have come to the wrong place. But if you want entertaining, real-world, tried-and-true examples of amazing business innovations, then keep reading.

The best way to learn and understand what it takes to innovate is by looking at people who have done it. In *The Big Idea*, you have the real-life stories of 30 different products that were truly unique, started as an idea in someone's head, and went on to become household names. How did Procter & Gamble invent and market the world's first disposable diapers, Pampers? How did Dr. Spencer Silver turn his mistake in the lab, a glue that wasn't very sticky, into Post-it Notes? Did you know that the guy who invented the Palm Pilot had tried two previous times to create a handwriting software recognition device?

Here are the stories of real people—some in large corporations, some working on their own—who had a brainstorm one day, a eureka! moment, and then somehow figured out how to turn that idea into a global product or brand. These lessons are important, not just for entrepreneurs, but for anyone who wants to be more innovative. Chris Haney and Scott Abbot were two Canadian journalists that loved to play Scrabble. When they realized that Scott had bought six games of Scrabble over the course of his life because those little tiles have a tendency to get lost, the two friends decided to invent a board game. The fact that a successful new board game hadn't been invented for 50 years didn't matter. Trivial Pursuit was the result of their efforts, but it wasn't created before one of the men almost had a nervous breakdown and both almost went bankrupt. In the end, they—and the friends and family who invested in their dream—became millionaires.

Living the dream is what creating a great product is all about. Bobby Kennedy once said, quoting George Bernard Shaw, "Some men look at things that are and ask 'Why?' I think of things that never were and ask 'Why not?'" If ever there were an axiom for the innovative entrepreneur, this would be it. For a product to become wildly successful, someone must have an idea stuck in his or her head—a new idea about a new thing that simply won't go away. The burning desire to see it through, to make real what is just a thought, is the juice that drives the innovator.

Great innovators have other traits in common as well. They are persistent, may fail more than once, but like the Energizer Bunny, they keep going and going. Earl Tupper spent his life tinkering and creating mostly worthless products before he created a new type of plastic and invented Tupperware. If risk-taking is a trait shared by all entrepreneurs, the entrepreneur who hitches his wagon to an innovative star is in a risk-taking class by himself. Al Neuharth bet the considerable resources of Gannett Publishing on his belief that a national, general interest daily newspaper would fly. *USA Today* is the result of that risk.

These rags-to-riches stories of risk rewarded are, all at once, enlightening, fun to read, interesting, and useful. They pave a path that others can venture down and, in the process, teach people how *not* to make some of the same mistakes. By the same token, these stories can show you what works and what doesn't. Years of hard knocks can be avoided. But that's not all. What I have endeavored to do in this book is to put these tales of business innovation in context. Each chapter, therefore, revolves around a theme. What do the cell phone, the new Volkswagen Beetle, the computer mouse, and Prozac all have in common? If you read Chapter 6, you will learn that all faced enormous resistance and almost never came to be. In Chapter 8, all 30 of these disparate tales are woven together, and the lessons of these pioneers become accessible.

Innovators like these people are all around us, and the ideas they are working on today may well be the products you use tomorrow. In San Francisco, Stone Melet is creating a product that could make the Internet a much easier place to visit. Melet was an up-and-coming television news anchor/reporter when the innovation bug bit him. His idea: To create a better way for Web sites to gather information from their visitors. Melet and his cofounders realized that almost every Web site had to send visitors to a page buried deep in the site if it wanted to gather user comments, answer a question, or get an e-mail address. There must be a better way. As a result of their questing, Askfor-free.com was born. Melet drafted a business plan, quit his television job, moved across the country, and, based on the power of his commitment and an equally powerful concept, was able to attract seven-figure venture capital (VC) funding and some top-tier angel investors. The "AskBox"

Melet is developing will enable Web customers to interact with any site, without ever having to stop what they are doing and venture off to uncharted Web page territory. The AskBox may soon become as ubiquitous as the search feature now prevalent on so many sites.

Innovators can come in all shapes and sizes. In Los Angeles, Jeff Eichen is taking a different route. Rather than seek VC funds, Eichen is going it alone, much like many of the innovators in this book. Eichen's business is making novelty-based active sportswear for the Gen-X crowd. His innovation? All of his products are made from Astroturf. Turf-Boy USA is developing a popular line of turf clothing, mostly golf-related items, and turf accessories. At Turfboy-USA.com, you can buy Astroturf golf caps, golf bags, golf shoes, cowboy hats, wallets, and, their bestseller, Astroturf coasters. Not interested? Your son sure is.

Finally, in Portland, Oregon, Ed Rockower and Paul Fogel are innovating in an altogether different way. Fogel spent years working as a hospital administrator. He learned that hospitals have a difficult time analyzing profits and losses, because there is often too much data. So Fogel decided to build a better mousetrap. In two weeks, on his own and at night, he created a revolutionary, powerful computer program that would enable hospital administrators to quickly and easily analyze the business of illness. Fogel then spent the next four years refining the program. But even then he needed help like many of the innovators you will read about in this book. Many innovators are inspired inventors, but not all have the business acumen necessary to get their product to market. Chester Carlson was brilliant enough to invent what would later become the Xerox machine but couldn't sell his idea to anyone until he teamed up with Joe Wilson. So Paul Fogel needed his Joe Wilson and found him in Ed Rockower. Together, Rockower and Fogel are turning their innovative product and their company, Executive Information Systems, Inc. (www.eisorg.com), into a leader in hospital database management.

Innovation can come at any time and in many forms. The innovative product can come from within a corporation or in an eccentric's garage. Whatever the case, the fascinating "rest of the story" tales in this book will not only entertain you but also will enable you to avoid mistakes, get ahead, and just maybe change the world.

Acknowledgments

The author would like to thank his beautiful, smart, funny wife, Maria, for all of her help and support. Lilli was also a valuable inspiration in the preparation of this book. Sydney was her usual delightful self, and Mara was great, as always. Thanks, too, to Spence for his ideas, humor, and great suggestions. Comments and suggestions by Raphael were also very helpful. I would also like to thank the many people who helped me compile these great stories, including John Mitchell, Jonathon Kreissman, Judy Schuster, Elizabeth McKinley, Ed Rider, Jay Baldwin, Kinney Thiele, Donna Lipari, Glen Bozarth, and Blair Austin. Finally, Thanks to Mary B. Good and everyone at Dearborn Trade Publishing for making this book possible.

Dreaming the Impossible Dream

Innovation that sells is a rare commodity. Creating a product that speaks to people, fulfills a market need, and becomes a necessary and useful item is the rare sort of business home run that companies live for. For every Post-it Note, there are a hundred bagel slicers that never survive the prototype stage.

There is no shortage of obstacles to creating the magic product. Whether it is convincing the "suits" that the idea merits further discussion (let alone a budget) or whether the idea is so cutting-edge that consumers don't even know they need it, turning innovative ideas into innovative products is no easy task. Before the innovator can even get the money to go forward, before it can be determined if there might be a market for the product, he or she must decide if it is feasible. For the creative mind, new ideas are not always that hard to come by. The challenge is in turning the idea into a product that the public understands, is technologically feasible, and is profitable. Taking a novel notion and turning it into a profitable product is one of the trickiest feats the business innovator will encounter.

Vive la France
The Story of Teflon

On April 6, 1938, a 27-year-old DuPont scientist named Roy J. Plunkett was working on developing a new chlorofluoro-carbon for use as a refrigerant. He had planned to take some tetrafluoroethylene (TFE), which is a gas at room tempera-ture, and synthesize it with hydrochloric acid. Plunkett and his assistant, Jack Rebok, prepared 100 pounds of TFE and, for safety's sake, stored the canisters in dry ice overnight.

The next day, Rebok connected a canister of TFE to the reaction apparatus, opened the valve, and nothing hap-pened. Had the gas somehow leaked out? Rebok and Plun-kett weighed the cylinder and found that the gas was still inside. Plunkett removed the valve completely, turned the canister upside down, shook it, and some white flecks of powder floated out. Plunkett and Rebok then sawed open several of the canisters and, to their surprise, discovered that the interior walls were lined with a smooth, waxy white coating. Something about the combination of pressure and temperature had forced the TFE molecules to join together. Plunkett wrote in his lab notebook: "A white solid material was obtained, which was supposed to be a polymerized product."

The two men began to analyze the new material and found it to be quite extraordinary. In his notebook, Plunkett noted that it "melts at a temperature approaching red heat, burns without residue." More interestingly, it was impervi-ous to freon, ether, petroleum, alcohol, sulfuric acid, glacial acetic acid, nitric acid, mold, and fungus. Further tests showed that water did not cause it to rot or swell, and expo-sure to sunlight did not degrade it. After successfully re-creating what had occurred by chance inside the canisters, Plunkett applied for, and received, a patent in 1941.

For the next three years, DuPont experimented with ways to safely produce PTFE (polymerized TFE) in industrial quantities. The happenstance method that Plunkett and Rebok had stumbled on proved to actually be highly dangerous, leading more than once to explosive reactions because of the heat released in the process. Experiments eventually led to a feasible, if costly, procedure. Meanwhile, DuPont also began identifying the properties that would make PTFE a marketable product. The most promising was its resistance to electric currents and most chemical reactions, which would certainly be useful in industrial applications. But, a commercial use for the substance was nowhere in sight.

The advent of World War II solved the immediate problem, allowing DuPont to concentrate on industrial uses. Scientists working on the Manhattan Project needed equipment that would stand up to the highly corrosive uranium gas necessary to create part of the first atomic bomb. PTFE fit the bill, and DuPont agreed to reserve its entire output for government use. For security reasons, PTFE was referred to by a code name, K 416. The Manhattan Project consumed about two-thirds of DuPont's PTFE output; the remainder was used for other military applications. The substance was also ideal for the nose cones of bombs, because it was both electrically resistive and transparent to radar. It was also used in airplane engines, in explosives manufacturing, for radar systems in bombers, and as a lining in liquid-fuel tanks, whose cold temperatures made less sturdy linings brittle.

As the war wound down, DuPont decided to go ahead with researching commercial applications for its miracle substance. Needing a name, they decided to expand the word TFE and call the substance Teflon. No other product on the market was as resistant to corrosion, and none was anywhere near as durable or maintenance-free. But the company faced significant obstacles. Because its melting point was so high, Teflon could not be easily molded. Further, and significantly, DuPont chemists faced the problem of trying to make the greatest nonstick substance ever invented stick to another surface.

Research led to several usable forms of Teflon. Teflon granules allowed the substance to be compressed and baked into blocks. Teflon powder could be blended and used to coat wires and make tubing. "Aqueous dispersions" were used to make enamels that could be sprayed or brushed onto a surface and then baked in place. Sheets of Teflon could be attached to other items with screws. Machine parts could be immersed in a layer of Teflon powder. Most methods required repeated applications to build up a film that was thick enough. Teflon was used for gaskets, valves, pumps, and bearings.

By 1949, Teflon was also being used in commercial food processing. Teflon-lined bread pans and muffin tins became standard equipment in many bakeries, and in candy factories, Teflon was used to coat conveyor belts. A 1953 DuPont television commercial showed a Teflon-coated bread pan that had "baked 1,258 loaves of bread and . . . never had a drop of grease in it." But at this point, DuPont hit the brakes. The first draft of the script for this commercial predicted that skillets would be soon coated with Teflon, but that line was deleted before the commercial was filmed.

DuPont was hesitant to market Teflon-coated cookware for home use due to concerns that it might lead to injuries and lawsuits. Tests showed that Teflon might soften at 620 degrees Fahrenheit, which was a problem because stovetops could exceed that level. Moreover, frying pans were usually made from aluminum and DuPont had yet to devise a method of firmly attaching Teflon to aluminum. Researchers also found that adequate ventilation was required because at high temperatures, small quantities of gaseous decomposition products were released, although the fumes given off by overheated Teflon pans were less toxic than those given off by heated cooking oil. For these reasons, DuPont decided to proceed with caution.

Enter Marc Grégoire, a French engineer. Grégoire had a friend who had, in fact, figured out a way to affix Teflon to aluminum. His process involved covering the aluminum with acid to create a microscopically pitted surface, coating the surface with Teflon powder, and heating it to just below its melting point, thereby causing the Teflon to meld to the aluminum surface. This process created a Teflon that could not be melted. Grégoire decided to coat his fishing gear with Teflon to prevent tangles. Liking the results, his wife Colette thought that they should try to coat her cooking pans. Grégoire agreed to try it and, after much experimentation, loved the results, and was eventually granted a French patent in 1954. In 1955, the Grégoires set up a business: Marc coated pans in their kitchen and Colette sold them on the street to French chefs who, despite their love of tradition, snapped them up.

The Grégoires formed the Tefal Corporation in 1956 and opened a factory. Soon thereafter, French health officials declared Teflon-coated frying pans to be safe. In 1958, the French agriculture ministry approved the use of Teflon in food processing. That year, the Grégoires sold one million skillets. Two years later sales approached three million.

The success of this development was not lost on DuPont. The company decided to seek the approval of the U.S. Food and Drug Administration (FDA) for the use of Teflon in cooking. The company redoubled its efforts to test frying pans and other cooking surfaces under extreme conditions. In 1960, the company gave the FDA reams of data, collected over nine years, on the effects of Teflon in the kitchen. Within a few months the FDA decided that the resins did not "present any problems." But even so, and despite the gold that the Grégoires had mined from Teflon in France, DuPont continued to move slowly; marketing Teflon-coated cookware was simply not a priority.

Enter Tom Hardie. Hardie had met Marc Grégoire during a business trip to France in 1958, and the Frenchman told Hardie about his business and the factory he was building. After returning to the States, Hardie concluded that Teflon cooking pans might sell well in the United States, yet Grégoire was reluctant to do business with an American. But because money helps people overcome most opposition, before long Hardie had secured the rights to manufacture nonstick cookware using the Tefal process. Hardie spent the next two years trying to peddle the idea of Teflon-coated cookware to manufacturers, but was wholly unsuccessful. Nonstick pans were too new. Discouraged but not defeated, Hardie decided to buy 3,000 pans from his French counterpart. On receiving the first-ever shipment of Teflon-coated frying pans in the United States, Hardie stored his catch in the barn on his sheep farm in Maryland.

Two hundred department stores later, he received not a single order. Nothing if not persistent, Hardie then met with executives at DuPont and was able to convince them that cookware could be a valuable new market for them. With the giant company now on his team, Tom Hardie was finally able to meet the Macy's buyer. Hardie met in George Edelstein's tiny basement office in New York City and Edelstein placed a small order. On December 15, 1960, the first Teflon skillets went on sale for $6.94 at Macy's Herald Square store. The pans quickly sold out. Hardie then met with Roger Horchow, a buyer for Neiman Marcus. Horchow agreed to test a sample skillet even though his store didn't have a housewares department, and gave it to a cookbook editor to try out. Of course, she loved it, and Neiman Marcus went on to sell 2,000 skillets in one week. Horchow later recalled, "Skillets were piled up, still in the shipping crates, as in a discount house, with the salesladies handing them out to customers like hotcakes at an Army breakfast." Hardie was soon swamped with orders and the inventory in his barn quickly evaporated. Grégoire was unable to meet the American demand (which reached a million pans per month in mid-1961), so Hardie built his own factory.

Unfortunately for Mr. Hardie, several major American cookware companies also decided to start making Teflon pans. Suddenly the market was saturated with nonstick cookware, and because the American companies had no experience with Teflon coatings, much of it was inferior. Just as quickly as the fad hit, it was gone. Nonstick pans had acquired a bad name. Warehouses were filled with unsold stock. Sadly, Tom Hardie had to sell his factory.

But DuPont still believed that the product had enormous potential. It commissioned research and discovered that the inferior cookware was the result of faulty production methods that turned out shoddy pans whose coatings scraped off much too easily. As a result, the company established coating standards for manufacturers and initiated a certification program. By 1968, DuPont had developed Teflon II, which not only prevented food from sticking to the pans but was also more scratch-resistant. Later generations of Teflon cookware with thicker coatings improved bonding.

Today, Teflon, the product that once had no commercial value, can be found almost anywhere you look in the home. Besides ubiquitous cookware, Teflon has been found to be, not surprisingly, a fantastic water repellent that is used to repel water and prevent stains in carpet, apparel, home fashions, and furniture. As a fiber, Teflon is used in socks to reduce friction and blisters.

As for the Grégoires, their Tefal cookware remains the industry standard. There really is something to be said for the first mover's advantage.

Innovators come in all forms. Some, like the scientists at DuPont, have a scientific bent. Many are fairly eccentric loners who search long and hard for a solution to a perceived problem, while others stumble on something new and figure out a way to make a buck off it. Yet while they may differ in temperament, what all innovators share is a vision. The best of all possible worlds is when the visionary innovator has the resources at his or her disposal to make his or her impossible dream a reality. Commander Eugene F. McDonald was just such a man.

Lazy Bones Jones
How the Remote Control Came to Be

If men knew of Eugene McDonald and Dr. Robert Adler, and most don't, they would almost universally want to thank them for their invention. Born in Syracuse, New York, McDonald was an entrepreneur from an early age—his first business was repairing electric doorbells when he was in high school. In 1912, he created another company to finance car purchases on time payments, a first in the auto industry. But what McDonald really enjoyed was electronics. In 1918, after a stint in World War I as a naval commander, McDonald and two friends—all three wireless-radio enthusiasts—set up shop on a kitchen table in Chicago and began making radio equipment for other amateurs. In the early 1920s, the men started their own amateur radio station with the call letters 9-ZN, inspiring a name for their electronics business. 9-ZN soon became 9-ZNith. In 1923, the Zenith Radio Corporation was incorporated with McDonald as its first president, a position he would hold for 45 years.

The young company grew quickly, innovating mostly in the area of radio engineering. Its early accomplishments included the world's first portable radio (1924), the first home radio receiver to operate on household current (1926), and the first automatic push-button radio (1927). Zenith even pioneered AM and FM radio broadcasting—including the invention of the stereo FM radio broadcast system. The company soon branched out into other areas, especially the nascent television field, where McDonald's vision would come to the fore. McDonald soon formed and became the first president of the National Association of Broadcasters. He was also instrumental in the establishment of the Radio Commission, which later became the Federal Communications Commission.

Despite his enviable success in radio, what men will remember Commander McDonald for are his innovations in the area of television and television broadcasting. Not only did he develop the first prototype television receivers in the late 1930s, but in 1948, he and Zenith introduced one of the first-ever black-and-white TV sets. Yet, while McDonald and his company were leaders in television technology, he detested the use of commercials to pay for broadcasting. Commander McDonald believed that television viewers would not tolerate commercials and was convinced that sooner or later commercial television would collapse. It was his ardent goal, his dream, his vision, to rid viewers of annoying television commercials.

His first idea was to create subscription TV—a primitive cable network. But he was so far ahead of the curve that he was no longer even on the highway. Subscription television was an idea too far ahead of its time. Instead, he began to devise a device that would allow viewers to change the station from a remote location when a commercial would come on. He had seen similar remote units in the military and decided to adapt the technology for television. While waiting for the development of commercial-free subscription television, Commander McDonald decided that what each man really needed was a remote control for his TV.

Because the commander had a company that had expertise in this area at his disposal, he instructed his top engineers to create a remote control device that would allow users to operate their televisions from the comfort of the living room couch. In 1950, the first television remote control, the "Lazy Bones," was developed and offered for sale.

While it was not really all the commander hoped it would be, it was a start. The hand-grenade-shaped Lazy Bones was connected to the TV set by a cable. By pushing buttons on the remote control, viewers rotated the channels higher or lower. Lazy Bones also included buttons that turned the set on and off. "Amazing!" trumpeted a Zenith ad. "Prest-o! Change-o! With Zenith's Lazy Bones you remain seated during an entire evening's television entertainment!" While the Lazy Bones was an innovative product, it was far from perfect. Consumers disliked the Lazy Bones because they had a tendency to trip over the unsightly wire that meandered across the living room floor.

McDonald was not a happy camper. Like Bobby Kennedy, he dreamed of things that never were and asked "Why not?" What Commander McDonald dreamed of was something truly unique, a consumer electronics product that did not exist—a wireless remote control. He wanted to develop a unit that was simple and easy to use that could ferret users away from commercials in an instant. He sent Zenith engineers back to the drawing board with their marching orders: Create a wireless remote that would enable viewers to turn the picture and sound on and off, change channels, and mute those blasted commercials.

A few years later, Eugene Polley, a Zenith engineer, thought he had solved the problem. His "Flashmatic" represented the industry's first wireless TV remote. Introduced in 1955, Flashmatic used a flashlight that the user would point at the TV. Inside each corner of the TV was a photo cell with a different control function: picture on in one corner, picture off in another, sound up in the third corner, and sound down in the other. Turning the dial on the remote clockwise and counterclockwise changed the channels. A 1955 ad in the *Saturday Evening Post* read: "To the magic of Christmas, add a bit of electronic magic from Zenith. Shoot off annoying commercials from across room with flash of magic light . . . No wires or cords! It's so astounding that you have to see it to believe it!" While the Flashmatic pioneered the concept of the wireless TV remote control, it had some severe limitations. It was a simple device that had no protection circuits and, most problematic, if the TV sat in the sun, it had a tendency to go bonkers.

While Commander McDonald loved the concepts proven by Polley's Flashmatic, it still was not what he envisioned, and he was not a person that you wanted to displease. He put one of his top engineers, Dr. Robert Adler, in charge of the product. McDonald, according to Adler, summoned "everyone who was everyone" at Zenith into his office. The direct order from the commander: Build me a better remote. Now.

"The obvious thing was to do it by radio waves," Adler recalls. "But radio goes through walls, and the feeling was that people in two different houses would control each other's TV. I just scanned in my mind all the things that couldn't go through walls. There are not many of them." One idea that Adler and his engineers came up with was to use sound, but they eventually concluded that sound too had its limits, namely, people might not like hearing a noise every time they operated their remote control. Moreover, the engineers thought that it would be difficult to find a sound that wouldn't accidentally be duplicated by either household noises or by the sound coming from TV programming.

After much discussion and experimentation, Adler finally settled on ultrasonics, or high-frequency sound. He and his engineers initially chose 18,000 cycles per second, a frequency that was supposed to be too high to be heard by a human ear. But a young woman on his team could hear that sound, and complained. "It made her jump," Adler chuckles. "She threatened to quit, so we changed the frequencies. We wanted to keep her." Once they solved that issue, the Zenith engineers had an even higher bar to leap. Among the dictates that they had been given was this unusual one: The remote could not be operated by batteries. The Zenith sales staff felt that if the battery went dead, the customer might think something was wrong with the TV. Because the remote control didn't emit light or show any other visible signs of functioning, people might think it was broken once the batteries died.

But even this difficult request did not stop our hero, Dr. Adler. He and his staff ingeniously created a remote control by using lightweight aluminum rods. These rods, when struck at one end, emitted distinctive high-frequency ultrasonic sounds, sort of like a piano key hitting a wire to produce a note. The unit used four rods, each approximately 2½ inches long: one for channel up, one for channel down, one for sound on and off, and one for set on and off. Each rod was slightly different in length, therefore emitting a slightly different sound. The trigger mechanism was similar to the trigger of a gun. It stretched and then released a spring that struck a small hammer that then struck the end of the aluminum rod, creating a high-frequency pitch. Batteries were not included because batteries were not needed.

Finally, Zenith engineers had created what Commander McDonald dreamed about for so many years. By the fall of 1956, the Zenith "Space Command" was offered for sale, becoming the first-ever practical wireless remote control device. Sleek and sharp, the Space Command, according to a Zenith ad from the era, was "the first true remote control unit for Televisions! It answers silent commands from your easy chair . . . or even from the next room. Turns set on and off, changes stations, mutes sound, shuts off long annoying commercials." (The commander's dream come true!) Moreover, the Space Command needed "No wires, no cords, no batteries, no radio control waves, no flashlights, no transistors!"

Like any innovative product that makes a difference, the Space Command did a few things very well, and for that reason, it was a popular product for a long, long time. Although subsequent Space Commands used vacuum tubes, by the early 1960s, transistors began to replace the bulky tubes. In this modified form, Dr. Adler's ultrasonic remote control technology was an unqualified hit, remaining in use for over 25 years. Its run ended in the early 1980s, when the industry moved to infrared remote controls, but not before more than 9 million ultrasonic remote controls had been sold.

Dr. Adler's invention changed the way people lived, and changed the electronics industry forever—99 percent of all TV sets, and 100 percent of VCRs sold in this country come with remote controls. According to the Consumer Electronics Association, the average American household has at least four remotes. Most of these operate televisions and stereos, but remote controls have expanded their domain to include other areas of the house: garage doors, fireplaces, ceiling fans, air conditioners, house lights, and window blinds. "The remote represents power." says Ron Simon, curator of television at the Museum of Television and Radio in New York.

According to a survey by the Television Institute: 34 percent of us have fallen off the sofa while reaching for the remote; 25 percent of us reach for the remote with our feet or toes; 53 percent of us would rather have someone throw the remote across the room than get up and get it ourselves; and 60 percent of us take the batteries out of another appliance to keep the remote working. The remote has become so important to the American male, that in 2000, *Sports Illustrated* dubbed Dr. Adler and Eugene Polley (the inventor of the Lazy Bones) the magazine's Men of the Millennium.

As for Dr. Adler, he owns only one remote, which he uses sporadically, because, at age 86, he has better things to do than watch TV. "Until a few months ago, I had a 20-year-old TV set and remote control," he says. "John Taylor [public relations spokesman for Zenith] decided this was a situation that could not be tolerated and they presented us with a beautiful new TV set and matching remote." He admits, however, "I don't use it enough to be really familiar with it. But I know how to turn it on and off."

On very rare occasions, a big idea strikes an innovator and he or she has the resources available to see it through to completion. In the real world, most business innovators don't have discretionary multi-million-dollar budgets that can be utilized to test the mere feasibility of an idea, let alone the millions more it might take to get that idea to market. Far more often, the intrepid inventor gets a brainstorm that so strikes his fancy that he then spends his own time and money in dogged pursuit of an idea that won't leave him alone. Sometimes the dream is made of pipe, and happily sometimes it is spun from gold.

Velcro
Re-creating Nature's Velvet Crochet

The herb burdock has proven to be both a blessing and a curse to humanity. On the positive side, burdock has long been considered a medicinal herb. Chinese herbalists recommend the use of burdock for colds, measles, and as a mild laxative. Burdock is also incorporated into herbal cancer treatments in various cultures. And for centuries, the root of burdock has been used as a blood purifier, helping the liver and kidneys eliminate waste. Seventeenth century herbalist, Nicholas Culpeper, even promoted a rather unusual regimen for expectant mothers using the leaves of burdock. Culpeper's recommendation: "By its [burdock's] leaf or seed you may draw the womb which way you please, either upward by applying it to the crown of the head in case it falls out; or downwards in fits of the mother, by applying it to the soles of the feet; or if you would stay it in its place, apply it to the navel, and that is a good way to stay the child in it."

Yet despite all of the surprising benefits of burdock, you are likely more aware of its negative qualities if you have ever taken a walk in the woods. Burdock, more commonly known as a burr, has a nasty habit of sticking to socks and dogs. And pulling burrs from both is often the least enjoyable part of a hike. That is, unless you are George de Mestral, a man who turned that seemingly unwelcome task into a multi-million-dollar business, a feat which may not be all that surprising when you consider that he received his first patent at age 12 for designing a toy airplane. Born in 1907 in a small village in the wine region of Lake Lèman, near Lausanne, Switzerland, de Mestral grew up on an estate that his family had owned for several centuries. Through odd jobs, he paid his way through one of the best colleges in Europe, the Ecole Polytechnique Federale de Lausanne, Switzerland, where he graduated as an electrical engineer.

After graduation, de Mestral went for a walk in the woods with his dog near his home. He wanted to catch some damselflies for viewing under a new microscope he had recently purchased, but was unable to catch any. The only thing he was able to catch was scores of sticky burrs. As he didn't have any damselflies to view, de Mestral decided to look at the burrs under his microscope to see what made them stick. He found that each burr was covered with hundreds of tiny "hooks" that grabbed on to anything with a loop, such as clothing fiber, animal fur, or even human hair.

Those tiny hooks gave de Mestral an idea. If he could figure out a way to duplicate the hooks and loops found in microscopic nature, he could create a new product that could fasten things together without the use of a zipper or button. He knew that he would need to create two different sorts of fabrics to build on the clue he had found in nature. One would be similar to the burr—with hundreds of tiny, grabbing hooks. The other would need to have hundreds of tiny, catching loops. And so his quest began.

Being a visionary is not often an easy thing. The very nature of innovation is that the innovator sees something extraordinary where others see only ordinary. In fact, he or she sees things that others don't see at all. What the innovator calls a breakthrough—an event to be reckoned with—others may call a waste of time—a distraction to be avoided. Such was the fate of George de Mestral. As he took his idea around Lyon, France (which, at the time, was a worldwide center for weaving), people scoffed. Although many of the experts de Mestral spoke with were intrigued by the concept of a hook-and-loop fastener, all concluded that the idea just was not feasible. How could they duplicate hundreds of tiny hooks and loops on a small piece of fabric? At the time, there were no machines capable of duplicating what was found in nature—the loops were far too small and the hooks impossible to re-create.

De Mestral persistently continued, and finally found one expert who was willing to try to re-create the burr's hooking mechanism. Working by hand on a small loom, the weaver made two cotton tapes that, when pressed together, fastened just as strongly as Mother Nature's burrs. Unfortunately, the cotton he used proved to be a poor material because it quickly wore out. Undeterred, de Mestral then turned to synthetic materials. Years would pass as he experimented with a variety of fabrics, trying to find the right material. Finally, after a grueling process of trial and error, de Mestral found that nylon, when sewn under hot infrared light, formed durable loops.

But that was just the beginning. He also had to create the hooks by machine. The logistics of attaching hundreds of tiny perfectly sized hooks to tape delayed de Mestral's work for another eight years. Mechanizing the production process of weaving 300 matching hooks and loops proved nearly as difficult as finding the right fabric. While trial and error showed that nylon thread, woven in loops and then heat-treated, retained shape and resiliency for long periods, the trouble was that each loop had to be cut at just the right point to form a point that would fasten and unfasten again and again. Sometimes the loops were too big for the hooks, sometimes the hooks were too big for the loops.

With his money and enthusiasm almost gone, de Mestral, in another flash of inspiration, hit on a solution. He bought a pair of barber's shears and brought them to one of the weavers he had been working with. With the clippers, he snipped off the tops of the loops, thereby creating little nylon hooks exactly the right size to perfectly match the loops. This, he explained, was exactly what he needed—a loom that snipped loops after it wove them. He spent another year developing the loom. In all, it took George de Mestral ten years of determined effort to create a machine process that actually worked.

With his product finally ready to be taken to market, de Mestral needed a name for his hook-and-loop fastener. He liked the sound "vel" from the French word for velvet, *velour,* and "cro" from the French word for hook, *crochet,* and the name Velcro stuck, kind of like those annoying burrs. With the support of a strategic partner, de Mestral began Velcro S.A. in Switzerland. Velcro S.A. received its first patent in

France, covering "the invention and fabrication of special napped piles of man-made material at least some of these loops having the means of hooking near their ends."

Growth of Velcro was phenomenal from the start. Within a few years, de Mestral obtained patents and began to open shop in Germany, Switzerland, Great Britain, Sweden, Italy, Holland, Belgium, and Canada. By 1957, a mere five years after starting his company, de Mestral branched out to the United States and began American Velcro, Inc. (soon to be Velcro U.S.A.), based in the textile center of Manchester, New Hampshire. Today, Velcro sales exceed $100 million a year with customers in almost every industry.

Called one of the most useful inventions of the 20th century, Velcro can be found in the most unusual places. It held together a human heart during the first artificial heart surgery. It's used in nuclear power plants and army tanks, holding flashlights and tools to walls. NASA even uses it on the inside of space helmets to provide astronauts a rough surface on which to scratch an itchy nose or chin. Automobiles depend on Velcro to bond headliners, floor mats, and speaker covers. In the home, Velcro is used for pleating draperies, holding carpets in place, and attaching upholstery to chair and couch frames. And, of course, David Letterman proved that with enough Velcro, a man could be hurled against a wall and stick. George de Mestral (1907-1990) was inducted into the National Inventors Hall of Fame for his invention of Velcro.

Business innovation comes in two forms. Either someone gets a creative idea and diligently sees it through to fruition, as George de Mestral did, or an item is created by happenstance, such as Teflon. In that latter scenario, what to do with the product is not always clear. When the creation comes about by accident, in the lab for example, not only must someone realize that it is special, *and* decide what to do with it, *and* figure out how to make a buck off it, *and* fund it, he or she must adopt the invention and champion it as well. That is a lot of *ands*. But given the right creation, it can be well worth the effort.

From Radar Waves to the Radar Range
The Surprise Discovery of the Microwave Oven

The Second World War began on September 1, 1939, when Germany invaded Poland utilizing a new type of combined operations tactics called blitzkrieg. Using this method, Poland was captured in just 28 days. On April 9, 1940, the same blitzkrieg tactics were used to quickly overtake Denmark and Norway. On May 10, 1940, Germany attacked Belgium, Holland, Luxembourg, and France, with the same results. Germany's sights then fell on England. Starting on July 10, 1940, the German Luftwaffe began to attack British shipping ports. The Battle of Britain had begun. The German attack focused heavily on British radar installations, damaging most of them severely. In the midst of this, British Prime Minister Winston Churchill put out a call for help to Britain's allies. A new radar system was needed, and quickly. Among those who heard his cry was Dr. Percy Spencer, a scientist employed by a small company in the States called Raytheon.

Spencer suggested a radical solution: The radar should be made using magnetron tubes. This, Dr. Spencer said, would not only simplify production, it would also improve the radar's performance. Dr. Spencer theorized that because magnetron tubes produce microwaves, installing them in Britain's radar system would enable the British to spot Nazi warplanes on their way to bomb the British Isles, without detection. The use of microwaves was an unheard of radar concept at the time. Initially considered too small to be in the running for the contract, Raytheon soon beat out giants such as Western Electric, RCA, and GE.

By 1942, Raytheon was in full war mode. Another one of its scientists, Fritz Gross, figured out a way to develop the microwave radar systems for use in the Navy, enabling American and British subs to spy on Nazi U-boats roaming the Atlantic. Raytheon also equipped U.S. PT boats with the radar (a feat other manufacturers previously claimed to be impossible), thereby enabling the Allies to see at night and to search and destroy enemy vessels.

After the war, as you might imagine, the demand for radars and magnetron tubes lessened considerably and Raytheon was looking to convert its wartime operations to the new peacetime economy. As part of this effort, Dr. Spencer experimented with the magnetron radars. It was then, in 1946, that Dr. Spencer (a self-taught engineer who obtained 120 patents in his lifetime) noticed something very unusual: The candy bar in his pocket melted. Intrigued, Dr. Spencer tried another experiment. This time he placed some popcorn kernels near the magnetron tube and, standing a little farther away, watched as the popcorn snapped, crackled, and popped all over his lab. Spencer was not sure what was causing this unusual turn of events, but was determined to figure it out. He decided to put the magnetron tube near an egg. Spencer and a colleague watched as the egg began to tremble. Again, they didn't have any idea what to expect; no one had ever seen such a phenomenon before. As the curious colleague moved in for a closer look, he got egg on himself in more ways than one. It was then that they discovered that low-density microwave energy produced by magnetron tubes cooked food.

One of the great things about being a research scientist is that you get to play around with intriguing ideas. Dr. Spencer continued to test ways to harness the power of the magnetron. He created a metal box with an opening at one end, into which he fed magnetron-induced microwave power. He then placed various foods in the box, turned the magnetron radar on, and waited. As expected, the temperature of the food rose very rapidly. Dr. Spencer had invented the microwave oven.

This was just the type of product Raytheon was looking for, and so a battery of engineers went to work on Spencer's new idea, developing and refining it. Within the year, the Raytheon Company had filed a patent for the microwave oven, and only a year later, in 1947, the first commercial microwave oven hit the market. These primitive units where gigantic and enormously expensive, standing 5½ feet tall, weighing over 750 pounds, and costing $5,000 each. Not surprisingly, most restaurants and other commercial food producers were highly reluctant to try this new oven. Between the expense, its size, and a general lack of understanding about microwave cooking, these first units found only limited acceptance. Initial sales were very disappointing. Only outfits like railroad cars and ocean liners, places where large quantities of food had to be cooked quickly, ordered the massive machines.

What Raytheon had on its hands was a lot of potential and not much more. Expensive and cumbersome, the first microwaves were far from being commercially viable. If innovation is a lot like genius, 1 percent inspiration and 99 percent perspiration, then Raytheon perspired a lot. Sending teams of engineers back to the drawing board, the company endeavored to figure out a way to make the product faster, better, and cheaper. The company hoped that the invention of a new air-cooled magnetron, which obviated the need for the plumbing that cooled the original, would prove to be the breakthrough that propelled the microwave to stardom.

But even improved, culinary experts disliked the oven's shortcomings. Meat refused to brown. French fries turned white and limp. Food was easily overcooked. On the other hand, these issues were less important in industrial applications. By having a microwave oven available, restaurants and vending companies were able to keep products refrigerator-fresh up to the point of service, then heat to order. The result? Fresher food, less waste, and money saved. Slowly, the convenience of the microwave began to overshadow its limitations.

As the food industry began to recognize the potential and versatility of the microwave oven, its usefulness was put to new tests as industries began to discover different uses for it—drying potato chips, roasting coffee beans, and roasting peanuts, for example. Meats could be defrosted, precooked, and tempered. Even the shucking of oysters was found to be made easier by microwaves. Other industries outside of food processing also soon found diverse applications for the microwave oven. In time, microwaves were being used to dry cork, ceramics, paper, leather, tobacco, textiles, pencils, flowers, wet books, and match heads. Before long, Raytheon's innovation had become a necessity in the commercial market and the possibilities seemed endless.

But it still was far from a mass commercial success. The Raytheon story illustrates another important lesson: Innovation often takes patience. In fact, it was decades from the time Dr. Spencer's chocolate bar melted until the microwave was refined to a point where it could be useful to the average consumer. It was not until Tappan introduced a scaled-down but still refrigerator-sized version in 1952, that microwave cooking was even considered for home use. Priced at $1,295, the new technology was accepted by only the wealthiest of families and, even then, with reservations regarding safety.

But Raytheon had something that Tappan didn't—the first mover's advantage. The first mover's advantage is this: When a company is the first on the scene with a new idea that works, that idea and that company have the chance to capture a significant market share. That head start enables the innovator to create a positive image and refine the product before competitors are even out of the gate. So although Tappan was the first to the residential market, Raytheon had been refining its microwave technology for years, and soon introduced its own version of the microwave for home use. Dubbed the "Radar Range" (now you know why), the unit retailed for just under $500 and was smaller, safer, and more reliable than any previous model.

Even so, it took a while for the Radar Range to be accepted. Whether a mass-produced consumer-oriented microwave oven would ever be commercially feasible remained in doubt for some time. This is often the case with an innovative product. Consumers who had never seen a microwave oven before didn't understand it and many myths and fears surrounding the mysterious new electronic ovens raised questions: Was it safe? Could you stand in front of it when it was on? Were you really "nuking" your food?

But slowly, as in the commercial arena, people began to enjoy the convenience that a microwave offered. Studies began to emerge attesting to the safety of the product, and by the 1970s, more and more people were finding the benefits of microwave cooking outweighed any perceived risks. Despite initial fears, no one was dying of radiation poisoning, going blind, or becoming sterile or impotent. As fears faded, and as people became familiar with a microwave's capabilities and limitations, a growing acceptance began filtering into consumers' kitchens. Myths were melting away, and doubt was turning into demand.

By 1973, sales of microwave ovens, for the first time, exceeded those of gas ranges. The following year, a reported

17 percent of all homes in Japan were cooking with micro-waves, compared to only 4 percent of the homes in the United States. Though within a few years, microwave ovens were adorning the kitchens in over nine million American homes, or about 14 percent. By 1976, the microwave oven became a more commonly owned kitchen appliance than the dishwasher, reaching nearly 60 percent, or about 52 million U.S. households. America's cooking habits were being drastically changed by the time-saving and energy-conserving convenience of the microwave oven. Once considered a luxury, the microwave oven had finally developed into a practical necessity for a fast-paced world.

Dr. Spencer's invention, born by mistake, developed into what it is today because Raytheon recognized its potential—a quicker way to heat food—and persistently refined and marketed it until consumers realized their need for it. It was this commitment to innovation that allowed the product to grow into a tool that millions of people use every day. Little did Winston Churchill know at the time that when he said, "Never . . . have so many owed so much to so few," he could have just as well been referring to the microwave oven as the Battle of Britain, which led to its creation.

It is not unusual for a radically innovative idea to be called a boondoggle by those less visionary. To quote Paul Simon, one man's ceiling is another man's floor. So the innovator must not only be a visionary, but a darn good salesman as well. His or her challenge is to bring other people on board and convince them that the idea makes sense and will be profitable. That challenge is all the more acute when the feasibility of the product itself is uncertain. Then the innovator not only has to explain why the new idea makes sense, but also that it can actually be accomplished.

The Great Pumpkin Center
Birthplace of *USA Today*

For some people, their children are the most important thing in the world. For others, it's love, or money, or health. But not so for *USA Today* founder and former Gannett Newspaper CEO Al Neuharth. To Neuharth, "winning is the most important thing in life." While not the most popular sentiment ever, it's not surprising considering that Neuharth entitled his autobiography *Confessions of an S.O.B.* If ever there was an unrealistic, impractical, wild, unfeasible, pie-in-the-sky idea, Neuharth's *USA Today* was it. At a time when newspapers across the United States were going out of business left and right, and when the print media was being upstaged by new electronic sources like CNN, Neuharth decided not only to *start* a newspaper, but a national one at that.

There had never been a general interest national paper in the United States before, for many good reasons. Aside from the ungodly expense of such a venture and the fact that tapping the market would be extraordinarily difficult (when was the last time you changed papers?), the logistics of publishing a national paper were unimaginable. How many reporters would you need to cover news stories from across the country? How many salespeople would you need to service regional and national advertisers? How could you print and distribute the paper in every city every day? Although the *Wall Street Journal* was a national daily, its focus was much more narrow, and during that time in the early 1980s, it was only distributed in larger cities. The same was true for the *New York Times.* Actually, putting out a general interest national paper available in every city across the United States was, to most experts, beyond a Herculean task. It was logistically impossible, financially unfeasible, and basically, ridiculously stupid.

Yet, while a national newspaper seemed a radical notion, to Neuharth it made perfect sense. He had been thinking and working along these lines for years, and had analyzed the market just as long. As a young man in 1952, he started a statewide sports newspaper in South Dakota, and in 1966, he helped launch a brand-new paper in Miami, called *Today*. So for Neuharth, the idea of starting something big from scratch was not uncommon. He said, "Like most dreams or visions, the notion of a new national newspaper didn't appear full-blown all at once. But once it got inside my head, it wouldn't go away. For more than ten years, it was coddled inside me."

By 1979, Neuharth was in a position to do something about his vision, his heretofore secret dream. At the time, Gannett, the company he ran, was a booming newspaper chain, publishing 81 papers around the country, with a staff of 4,000 reporters and editors, selling more than 3.6 million papers a day. Most of Gannett's holdings were highly profitable, albeit small and medium-sized papers, concentrating on local news in smaller cities. (Jack Germond, the legendary political writer who once worked for Gannett, described them as "a bunch of shitkicker papers.") Gannett had its first billion-dollar year in 1979, earning the company $135 million in profits and netting it a yearly gain of 19 percent. But Neuharth is a highly competitive guy and running a syndicate of middling papers, even if they were quite profitable, was not exactly the chairman's dream. So Neuharth figured if he paired Gannett's money and his vision, together they could go far.

The CEO first tipped his hand, if only slightly, in November 1979 at a routine budget meeting. There he inquired about the possibility of setting aside $1 million from the next year's budget for "research and development." When Gannett's CFO, Doug McKorkindale, inquired about what he had in mind, Neuharth replied, "I'm not sure, but our business is changing. If we want to stay in front, we've got to be building more. Maybe Super-TV. Maybe Sunday newspaper supplements. Maybe a national newspaper." McKorkindale was surprised. "How would the money be spent? Who will you hire? What will you explore?" Said the chairman, "Doug, I'll figure out how to spend it, you figure out how to budget it."

In actuality, Neuharth knew exactly how he was going to spend it. The first step in his now-gestating National Newspaper (NN) plan was to get some experts from within Gannett, some "young geniuses," to figure out if creating a national newspaper was even possible. If it wasn't, there was no point in continuing. So the chairman searched throughout his empire to find just the right people. After a short time, he tapped four hotshots and called them to his Cocoa Beach, Florida, estate, "Pumpkin Center." Assembled and curious were Larry Sackett, Tom Curley, Frank Vega, and Paul Kessinger, none older than 31 years, and each with a different area of expertise. Neuharth explained to them why they were assembled, what he was thinking, and what he wanted. He asked them to answer four questions: Could Gannett publish and print a national newspaper? Could they distribute and sell it? Could they design something unique? Would advertisers "get it"?

As with many innovations in this book, the NN project was carried out in secret; Neuharth so believed in his vision that he was afraid of someone stealing his idea, and his thunder. Not even the Gannett board of directors was told about the project in the beginning. Meeting in secret in a shabby cottage owned by Neuharth's wife a few blocks from Pumpkin Center, the private cabal was told by the chairman, "We've got to be realists. We may conclude that this dream is silly as hell . . . in which case, we won't go ahead with it." But Neuharth knew that being the syndicate that it was, Gannett had an inherent advantage. He told the group,

"When you look at a map of the United States you will find that Gannett has production and distribution facilities within two hours of at least 40 very big markets." That was a head start.

Having been given their marching orders, the men set about to figure out whether Neuharth's baby was even remotely possible. Working out of the small, hot cottage proved to be difficult, and as time passed, tempers often flared. The four men had distinctly different styles and temperaments, and the challenges before them were considerable. Because there had never been a general interest national newspaper in the United States before, there were no statistics to easily assimilate. How many papers could they realistically sell in a day? For that matter, how many could they actually publish in a day? Where would the paper be published and how could it be distributed across the United States every single day? Was there even a market for a national paper? In a memo, Kessinger wrote, "We can do projections and assumptions and analyses and studies until hell freezes over, but we won't be able to answer 'yes' or 'no' . . . until we have a concept."

So creating a concept is what they did. Weeks dragged into months and the months dragged on. After numerous ideas had been rejected and many plans cast aside, they finally figured out how Gannett could feasibly publish a national newspaper simultaneously from Maine to Alaska. The answer was via satellite—at the time, a revolutionary concept. Says Sackett, "We had printing sites in many of the major markets. The technology was certainly there to transmit pages via satellite at a reasonable cost. So I was very encouraged that we had a good shot at pulling this off."

Step one settled, the Pumpkin Center gang then had to determine whether there would be any advertisers for a national newspaper. Their first answer was far from encouraging. While meeting with Gannett's advertising agency,

Sackett and Kessinger learned that national advertisers rarely advertised in newspapers. Major print advertisers advertised in national magazines because they required that their ads be in color. At the time, the United States' biggest newspapers, such as the *L.A. Times* for example, were produced on presses that had to run at high speeds for many hours, a process that practically precluded color. What Sackett and Kessinger learned that day was that if Gannett wanted national advertisers for its national newspaper, the paper would have to be printed in color. This idea was reinforced when a leading consultant to the magazine industry (with whom they met undercover) confirmed that national advertisers required color ads. Says Sackett, "I remember the two of us walking out and saying 'This sucker has got to be in color.'" Sackett and Kessinger flew to New York to give Neuharth the news: If he wanted a national paper, it had to be in color. Neuharth agreed that a color newspaper was the way to go, and, as Paul Harvey would say, "now you know the rest of the story." The country's black-and-white newspapers would never be the same.

Knowing now that a color paper distributed by satellite was the direction in which they had to head, the Pumpkin Center gang had to confront the fact that Gannett did not have enough offset presses to print *USA Today* in color, even if it were feasible to print a national newspaper in color. To do so would require an enormous outlay of money: Fixing or buying new printing presses, training people to use them, and the cost of color dye would require a considerable expenditure of capital. The man Gannett later tapped to make the technically impossible possible was Chuck Blevins. Blevins says, "There was not one person who we talked to who thought we could do it. I guess I was lucky enough that I didn't know we couldn't do it."

One thing the young bucks didn't have to do was figure out whether the paper could turn a profit. Their only charge was to determine if the project was feasible. Their answer after six months of undercover research? It was. The questions Neuharth began with were all answered in the affirmative. Gannett could produce and print a national paper, it could be distributed across the United States by satellite (though getting the paper from Gannett publishing houses to 100,000 sales outlets every single day would not be easy), readers would likely buy it, and, if it was in color, advertisers would advertise in it.

Delighted, the chairman proceeded full steam ahead, and all political obstacles fell by the wayside. Gannett's board of directors approved the plan and although the finance department was against it, there was not much it could do to stop steamroller Neuharth. In December 1980, Gannett announced its plans to produce and distribute a daily national newspaper. Most analysts saw the paper as a probable bust, an ode to Neuharth's ego, or both.

On the financial end, Gannett's finance staff was left to figure out how to make the thing profitable. Because there were no models to work from, coming up with legitimate business assumptions proved to be almost impossible. Much of the business plan had to be based, at least partly, on guesswork. How many copies would they sell? What would it cost to sell them? Says Kessinger, "[The finance guys] thought it was the craziest damn thing they ever heard of, they were just shaking their heads over these numbers." Their heads were shaking, because even in the most rosy of scenarios, the business plan showed *USA Today* with losses in the millions for years. Although Neuharth always changed the word *losses* to *investments,* the finance department was no less apoplectic. In the end, the business plan projected that it would be five full years before *USA Today* would be profitable, based on revenues of $250 million a year and circulation of more than 2 million. Fears that the new paper would financially cripple Gannett were very real.

The paper became a huge risk for all involved. Reputations and careers were on the line. Says Neuharth, "I told them that it would be a risky thing, and that there would be those who would be ready to pee on it the minute it was announced, and that there would be those who would be very gleeful if it didn't work." For Neuharth, if the paper went belly-up, it meant ending his career a failure. Similarly, for Gannett, the bet was extraordinary, both in terms of money and reputation. And for the myriad editors and writers who wagered their own reputations on their ability to create something radically new and innovative, the stakes were equally high. As Neuharth put it, "Anybody who is going to do this is going to feel that they have had the chance of a lifetime. We are going to expect that people will regard it as that and bust their tails and gamble on the long-term returns to them. And if we score, it will be very big."

Unfazed, Gannett forged ahead. To tap a more entrepreneurial spirit, small task forces were created and instructed to get the job done. Before long, prototypes began to emerge from the design department. Styles and fonts were adopted and abandoned. Editorial content and direction was created and discarded. Sports editors had to figure out how to cover every game played every night across the United States, and report the results in a timely fashion the next day. A key aim of everything they did was to be different, to distinguish this paper from the rest. It had to be snazzy, new, distinctive. Yet despite the chaos, the uncertainty, the insanity, of creating a national paper, everyone was enthused. Starting a newspaper from scratch was a rare opportunity indeed.

For Chuck Blevins, creating a color newspaper was incredibly difficult. By the summer of 1982, he was spending all his time in Gannett's noisy pressroom in Gainesville, Florida, in anticipation of *USA Today's* September 20 rollout in Atlanta. Blevins was trying to make Gannett's old printing presses print a clear color copy, without success. Test after test produced smeared pictures and out-of-focus color snapshots. Finally, a mere three weeks before the paper was set to launch, Blevins reluctantly concluded that there was no way this particular printing press would work. They needed a new machine. Goss, the world's largest manufacturer of the Urbanite printing presses Gannett needed, told Blevins it would take six weeks for delivery. Unacceptable, Goss was told. The next week, Goss delivered and installed the two huge machines. The tests were perfect, and a few weeks later, the first copies of *USA Today* rolled off the presses.

The first issue sold out. Throughout the United States, people were talking about and reading the new newspaper. If ever there were an overnight sensation (that took years to create), *USA Today* was it. On the mall in Washington, D.C., that first day, Neuharth was surrounded at a press event by Senate majority leader Howard Baker, Speaker of the House Tip O'Neil, and President Ronald Reagan. *USA Today* was, as the president put it, "a testimony to the kind of dreams free men and women can dream and turn into reality here in America."

The Innovation Rules

- The innovator must have a vision, often one not shared by others.
- Innovation without commitment dies on the vine.
- The first mover's advantage is real—and valuable.
- Sometimes, the innovator must be an SOB.

!!!!!!!!!!!!!!!!!!!!!!!!!

Radicals in Blue

Innovators face many challenges as they attempt to bring their great ideas to market. Internal problems, everything from a lack of corporate support to a lack of funding, can plague even the best ideas. And even when everything is in place on the home front, there is no shortage of external factors lying in wait to defeat the best brainstorms.

Among the latter is the possibility that a product might simply be too far ahead of the curve, too radical for its own good. This is a legitimate concern; creating a product that the public does not understand is dangerous indeed. Money can be wasted and time lost chasing a dream that is not allowed to mature. But it need not be so. As in Chapter 1, the products in this chapter reveal that creating a radically different product gives you the first mover's advantage. This in turn gives a company a head start on the myriad things required to turn an innovative idea into a business success—manufacturing, pricing, distribution, packaging, financing, consumer education, servicing, and so on. Being radical is not necessarily bad if it makes you first. Having an amazing new idea can change the world, at least, that's what Buckminster Fuller hoped.

Guinea Pig B
The Experiment That Created the Geodesic Dome

Buckminster Fuller was, among other things, the inventor of the geodesic dome. What is a geodesic dome you ask? Imagine Disney's Epcot Center. That beautiful, majestic, silvery, dappled dome made of interlocking triangles is a geodesic dome. On the playground, that unique dome play structure made from interconnected triangular bars is a geodesic dome. Geodesic domes have been turned into alternative lifestyle homes and camping tents, convention centers and movie theatres.

The dome can take on all of these different forms because structurally it is quite unique. Because it is a half sphere, and because spheres enclose the greatest possible volume using the least amount of surface, the geodesic dome, by the very laws of nature, encloses the greatest space using the least materials. It is the original "do more using less" idea. Construction of a dome requires about 60 percent fewer building materials than a conventional structure of the same size. As such, its inventor, whom *Time* magazine once called "the first poet of technology," argued that domes help save natural resources. The geodesic dome is also among the strongest structures on the planet (it is the *only structure* that gets stronger when made larger), while simultaneously being among the lightest, least expensive, and quickest and easiest to assemble.

To truly comprehend just how innovative, how radical, the geodesic dome is, look at the buildings around you. How many are built using corners and 90-degree angles? Your answer is likely "all of them." A geodesic dome uses no right angles. Not one. Or consider this story: A few years after Bucky Fuller invented the geodesic dome, the United

States Commerce Department had an emergency. The 1951 International Trade Fair was to be held that year in Kabul, Afghanistan. The Commerce Department's original plan was to send only a few exhibits. Then the U.S. government learned that its Cold War enemies, the Soviet Union and China, were sending huge exhibits. Not to be outdone, the United States Commerce Department needed to quickly send some large exhibits half way around the world, and it needed a structure to house them in once they got there. Constructing a conventional building would have been cost-prohibitive and too time consuming. After considering several options, the only viable solution was Buckminster's geodesic dome. Why? Only Bucky could meet all of the department's stringent requirements, including completing the 100-foot-diameter structure in a month, flying the structure to Afghanistan, assembling the structure using only a few people, and providing 8,000 square feet of display space. Because a geodesic dome can be put together using aluminum tubes, it fit the bill.

When the tubes and struts arrived in Afghanistan, the dome was erected in only a few hours by inexperienced workmen who spoke no English, but who understood how to fit the color coded hubs and struts together. Once completed, the dome was more popular than the exhibits it housed, and far more popular than the Russian and Chinese exhibits. The geodesic dome itself became an international hit. Within a few years, Henry Ford ordered one for the rotunda at Ford Motor's corporate headquarters, a 20-story dome housed the American pavilion at Montreal's Expo 1967 World's Fair, and the city of Long Beach, California, built one to house the Spruce Goose. All in all, not bad for a man who, in 1927, tried to kill himself.

Buckminster Fuller had always been something of a nonconformist. Smart of enough to get into Harvard, but stubborn enough to get thrown out—twice (the second time, legend has it, for blowing an entire semester's tuition on a date with eight chorus girls)—Bucky Fuller always wanted to do things his own way. But brought up in a patrician, Boston-educated, proper fashion, Fuller was also taught to get along and do what was expected of him. And so he did.

In the early 1920s, Fuller became part owner of a construction company known as Stockade Systems. Stockade created its own innovative product—a brick that weighed only two pounds, was unbreakable, and required no mortar. But as sometimes happens, Stockade's bricks were *too* revolutionary and threatened the establishment. Although Fuller was committed to innovation, Stockade couldn't afford to be. The company made no money because no one would buy the bricks, and Fuller was fired.

Bucky was soon hit with a second blow. His daughter Alexandra, who had suffered through polio, spinal meningitis, and pneumonia, among others ailments, finally succumbed and passed away. Fuller blamed himself for her death, concluding that had he been able to create (or afford) a less drafty home for them to live in, she would have survived. For Fuller, innovation was born of desperation.

On a cold night in Chicago in 1927, Buckminster Fuller decided to commit suicide. Walking out to Lake Michigan to drown himself, Fuller's life would change forever. He says that when he got to the lake, he suddenly found himself suspended several feet above the ground enclosed in a "sparkling sphere of light." Fuller recounted many times what he heard, "From now on you need never await temporal attestation to your thought. You think the truth. You do not have the right to eliminate yourself. You do not belong to you. You belong to Universe. Your significance will remain forever obscure to you, but you may assume that you are fulfilling your role if you apply yourself to converting your experiences to the highest advantage of others."

Needless to say, the experience changed his life. No longer could he work for others, just trying to get along. If he thought "the truth," then his job was to think and share. Fuller decided to trust his own judgment, an element that was missing in his life. He decided to rethink everything. As a result, for the next two years, he was silent, speaking to no one but his wife and baby daughter. When he came out of his self-imposed exile, Buckminster Fuller was a changed man. He decided to commit the remainder of his life to seeing how much one person could do to change the world for the better. His life would be an experiment and he would be the guinea pig, "guinea pig B" (for Bucky) as he called himself. Says Fuller, "In 1927, I resolved to do my own thinking and see what the individual, starting without any money or credit—in fact, with considerable discredit—with a wife and newborn child, could produce on behalf of his fellow men." His committed himself to learning the laws of nature and creating artifacts that utilized those laws.

He coined the term *Dymaxion* ("doing the most with the least") to describe this purpose. Compelled by the death of his daughter, Fuller was determined to put his best efforts toward creating structures that would house people more efficiently. His first invention was the Dymaxion house. This mast-and-wire construction, reflecting Fuller's nautical experience, was intended to be a technological solution to the American housing shortage of the Depression, but he never sold even one. His three-wheeled Dymaxion car was 20-feet long, weighed the same as a VW Beetle, got 30 miles per gallon, was steered by its single wheel *in the rear,* and could smoothly shuttle 11 passengers at 120 miles per hour. A fatal crash, wrongly blamed on the Dymaxion's steering instead of the other car, was also fatal to investors, and that project too failed.

Though a poor businessman, Fuller was clearly a new thinker, and increasingly received more and more attention.

This interest in his ideas led him to Black Mountain College in 1948. Black Mountain, a small, innovative school, had a summer program for visiting intellectuals, and invited Fuller to lecture and tinker for the summer. It was at Black Mountain that Fuller began to concentrate fully on a new form of geometrical architecture, having concluded that the traditional right-angle, squared configurations were unnecessary and not as nature intended. Instead, he was convinced that a more circular, triangular shape was the building block of nature and so should be for man. Fuller began to explore what would eventually become a new branch of mathematics, synergistic geometry. At the time, this was considered by most to be nonsense.

Almost four decades later, however, researchers at Rice University in 1985 discovered a new form of carbon—the basis of all life. Carbon-60, when magnified, is made up of interlocking triangles and looks exactly like a microscopic geodesic structure. The scientists who discovered the new carbon thus named it the "buckminsterfullerene." Dubbed a "Buckyball" for short, Carbon-60 is composed of 60 carbon atoms bound in a soccer ball shape arranged in 20 hexagons and 12 pentagons. In 1996, Robert F. Curl Jr. and Richard E. Smalley were awarded the Nobel Prize for their discovery of the buckminsterfullerene. The basis of life, it turns out, is in fact the geodesic form. Fuller was right.

His years of geometrical thinking had lead Fuller to conclude that it might be possible to create an octagonal-type structure using rods formed into interwoven triangles. Working with students, and two years' worth of mathematical calculations, Fuller was ready to create his first geodesic dome (a *geodesic* is the shortest line joining two points on a curved surface). At the end of the summer term at Black Mountain, Bucky Fuller and his crew attempted to build the dome. Confused onlookers only saw before them some aircraft tubing and joints sitting in the grass. But as the tubes were connected, and as the math proved to be correct, a strange-looking, spherical, triangular, dome-like structure took form. Taking only three days to build, this prototype 14-foot dome would become the basis from which all other domes were subsequently built. Covered with a vinyl plastic skin, not only was the dome erected quickly, but it was found to be incredibly strong and inexpensive to build.

Fuller knew that he had invented something truly revolutionary, and potentially, for the first time, highly commercial. The dome structure was unlike anything else being used in architecture and construction at the time. Though many around him were skeptical of its usefulness, Bucky Fuller exemplified a trait common to great innovators—he believed in his own product and knew that he needed to protect it. Accordingly, he took two important actions any innovator must take. First, he incorporated (as Geodesic, Inc.), and second, he applied for a patent.

A patent is issued by the United States Patent and Trademark Office and confers the right to exclude others from making, using, or selling the invention throughout the Unites States and its territories. A patent gives its owner a legal monopoly with regard to the patented invention for the life of the patent (the life of the patent varies depending on the type of patent). It is important to understand that an idea or suggestion cannot be patented. A complete description of the actual item to be patented is required. Knowing that major corporations might eventually try to usurp his invention, Fuller enlisted the help of the best patent attorney he could find, Donald Robertson. Robertson obtained a bulletproof patent for Fuller and it was soon impossible for anyone to create a geodesic structure without paying Fuller a license fee. Says Bucky, "If I had not taken out the patents, you would probably never have heard of me."

But protecting his idea was only the first step in getting his innovation to market. Fuller's problem was that the dome was so different that many people could not see its practical application. For years, Fuller had a difficult time utilizing and selling his fantastic structure. But a superior product can overcome many problems.

Fuller's first real break finally came after the Afghan sensation, when Henry Ford ordered a geodesic dome for Ford Motor's headquarters. That sale created the kind of publicity that can catapult a product to national prominence. The publicity surrounding the Ford dome also catapulted Fuller into America's consciousness for the first time. In May 1953, the prestigious *Architectural Forum*'s lead headline read, "Bucky Fuller Finds a Client!" The article stated, "The best architectural ideas and the best engineering ideas are stymied or too often discredited as screwball or dream stuff until someone is willing to back them with dollars. Take the case of Buckminster Fuller and his geodesic dome. For 20 years, everyone has said that some day somebody would revolutionize building by realizing Bucky's dreams. Ford was that man." The Ford dome's "photogenic structure was a public-relations man's dream" and was assembled in only 30 working days.

From that point on, with the backing of someone as influential as Henry Ford, and with the subsequent publicity heaped on Buckminster Fuller, orders for the geodesic dome began to flood in from all over the globe. A major purchaser was the United States government, using the domes for everything from protecting radar installations in the subarctic (it's the only structure that can withstand such conditions for long periods) to housing troops. Fuller was soon traveling the globe; building domes everywhere from Asia to South America, and lecturing to packed houses in between. His books became cult hits (*Operating Manual for Spaceship Earth*, for example), and in 1962, 40 years after being thrown out of Harvard a second time, Fuller was asked back as the Charles Norton Elliot Professor of Poetry. In

1965, Fuller appeared on the cover of *Time*. And in 1967, a huge, circular dome became the hit of the World's Fair in Montreal. After the success and publicity of the Montreal Expo, the once impoverished, suicidal, self-confessed "most successful failure ever," saw his income skyrocket to over $1 million a year, where it remained until he passed away in 1983.

During his lifetime, Buckminster Fuller wrote 28 books and was awarded 25 patents. Although he made his mark in areas as diverse as architecture, mathematics, religion, urban development, and design, he may be most fondly remembered as an optimistic futurist. Shortly before his death, he said: "Think of it. We are blessed with technology that would be indescribable to our forefathers. We have the wherewithal, the know-it-all to feed everybody, clothe everybody, and give every human on Earth a chance. We know now what we could never have known before—that we now have the option for all humanity to *make it* successfully on this planet in this lifetime. Whether it is to be Utopia or Oblivion will be a touch-and-go relay race right up to the final moment."

The geodesic dome lesson is illustrative on many levels. When a revolutionary new product is created, it is possible that people won't understand its usefulness. Because it is outside the realm of the ordinary and the understood, the radical idea can be lost if not nurtured. Nurturing that product becomes both the problem and opportunity that awaits the innovator. One must remain vigilant. It is the innovator's job to show the world that it needs what he or she has to offer. If you can do that, the world can be yours.

A Growth Industry
The Revolutionary Development of Viagra

Erectile dysfunction (ED) has always been a part of life, and cures have been sought for thousands of years. The ancient Chinese prescribed ginseng (meaning "man's root") to cure ED. In the Bible, Abimelech was stricken with ED for *thinking* about having sex with Abraham's wife. In ancient Egypt, ED was thought to be caused by an angry god and idol worship was the most common prescribed cure. In ancient Greece, the cure was a potion made from the scrapings of a knife used to geld rams. In the middle ages, the Catholic Church attributed ED to witchcraft and demonic possession. At the age of 16, King Louis XVI allegedly was unable to have intercourse with his wife Marie Antoinette. The diagnosis was excessively tight foreskin and his subsequent circumcision apparently cured his impotence. Folk remedies have always been offered as a cure—everything from crushed rhinoceros horns to pulverized antelope testicles have been used to try to solve this problem.

A different solution appeared shortly after 1961, when Geddings Osborn found that he was no longer able to have sexual relations with his wife of 30 years. Understandably upset with this turn of events, Mr. Osborn worked intently for the next few years in search of a solution to his dilemma. He developed a vacuum pump that caused an erection and was awarded a patent for his invention. While the pump does not provide the most romantic way to get an erection, it is still a popular product. Osborn Medical Systems continues to manufacture and distribute his Erecaid vacuum pump worldwide.

A better solution, however, was still desired, and as is often the case, one appeared by accident. In 1980, French physician Ronals Virag reported that during surgery on one of his patients, he inadvertently injected the man's penis with papaverine, thus relaxing what are known as the "smooth muscles" of the penile walls. This caused an unexpected, two-hour erection. ED researchers then began to experiment with injection therapy, pumping various drugs into the penis. Although phenoxybenzamine was found to produce an erection in a few minutes, the side effects of cardiac arrhythmia and hyperventilation were thought to be deterrents. Simultaneously, doctors in France, Japan, and the United States found that injections of papaverine, phentolamine, and prostaglandin E-1, the so-called tri-mix, could fairly consistently cure ED, at least temporarily.

Needless to say, having to self-inject one's penis was not always thought to be the best of plans, the cure being worse than the disease and all that. But many men, having tried the alternatives, injected away. The shots worked because the drugs relaxed the smooth muscles of the penis, thus allowing blood to flow in. Interestingly, after orgasm, the erection didn't always disappear, sometimes lasting for up to 90 minutes. The shots did have a high success rate—over 70 percent—and more than 500,000 men were soon injecting the tri-mix at $7 a pop.

With demand so high, clearly a better system was needed, and a doctor lost in a hospital would help find it. Dr. Jacob Rajfer, a urologist at the UCLA School of Medicine, had been studying impotence for years and believed ED was related to the failure of the smooth muscle in the penis to relax. As fate would have it, one day Dr. Rajfer got lost in the maze of identical halls that are the UCLA Med Center. He ended up in front of an office with a sign on it that read "Pharmacology: Smooth Muscle Lab" (to quote humorist Dave Barry, we are not making this up). Dr. Rajfer entered the lab and started chatting with one of the smooth muscle researchers who informed him that Dr. Louis Ignarro, the director of the Smooth Muscle Lab, had just discovered the long-sought-after cause of what makes the smooth muscles of the body relax. When nitric oxide (NO) comes into contact with smooth muscles cells, a chemical reaction takes place causing them to expand, or relax.

The two doctors decided to team up to test whether NO was present in the smooth muscles of the penis as well, and if so, whether it contributed to the erectile process. Very quickly they came to the realization that NO causes erections. At the same time, researchers for Pfizer Inc., the American pharmaceutical giant, were in Great Britain trying to determine a way to increase blood flow in the body because they hypothesized that this would ease the pain associated with a cardiac condition known as myocardial ischemia. They surmised that if they could increase blood flow to the chest, the patient might heal more quickly. But the drug they were testing wasn't working. Finally, as a last resort, they decided to noticeably increase the dosage of the drug, UK-92-480. They were able to get the blood flow to increase dramatically, although not to the organ they intended.

Of course, the Pfizer researchers quickly changed the focus of their research. The more they experimented with UK-92-480, the code name for the drug sildenafil, later given the brand name Viagra, the more they realized that they had stumbled on an oral cure for ED. Like Drs. Rajfer and Ignarro in California, the Pfizer team, lead by Dr. Ian Osterloh, discovered that NO helped cause erections by relaxing the smooth muscles.

This was remarkable, says Dr. Osterloh, because "in the past, the major reason we had trouble finding a drug that would cause an erection is that the penis contains blood vessels, but so do a lot of other organs in the body. So if a man took a drug that caused an erection by dilating blood vessels in the penis, it always caused dilation in the other parts of the body as well, many times with some very undesirable results." Sildenafil was remarkable because it worked only in the groin. The next step, as with any new drug, was to begin clinical trials. Medical history books are full of stories of promising medicines that failed when tested in double blind, random, two-way, crossover studies. The critical question to be answered by the studies was: Could Viagra keep it up?

If you think you have an idea for an innovative product but are dismayed by the cost of bringing it to market, be happy that you are not a pharmaceutical company, whose average cost, before FDA approval, is half a billion dollars per drug. But if the drug works, the company is rewarded with 20 years to exclusively produce and sell the drug. So to get to the pot of gold at the end of the rainbow, Pfizer would have to put its little blue pill through a battery of tests. Phase I is the smallest sampling, whereby the new drug is tried on a select group of patients, usually no more than a dozen. If that works, Phase II begins. At this stage, researchers are looking at safety and side-effect issues, so the groups are split in half, with part getting the drug and the others getting a placebo. In Phase III, hundreds are given the drug. By Phase IV, the drug is known to be effective and is being fine-tuned.

With Viagra, tests from the start were hard to beat. In Phase I, 12 men were given the drug, and remarkably, 10 of them were excited by the positive results. In Phase II, 90 percent of the men taking the actual drug reported significant improvement in their erectile functioning. The numbers stayed up in Phase III. Said one man to Dr. Osterloh, "The drug has given me back my life. It's changed the way I think about myself. I'm a new man." After the testing was completed, Viagra received rave reviews. One of the leading experts in ED, Dr. Raymond C. Rosen, said that the advent of Viagra "ushers in a whole new era."

On March 27, 1998, the FDA approved Pfizer, Inc.'s Viagra (sildenafil citrate) for use in the treatment of male erectile dysfunction. A flood of media attention the likes of which had not been seen since the release of the first HIV protease inhibitors in 1995, or Prozac in 1987, followed this event. Everyone was talking about Viagra, from *Saturday Night Live* to former presidential contender Bob Dole. Within two weeks of its introduction, Viagra became one of the fastest-selling drugs in the history of medicine. By April 1998, the drug's success was credited with pushing Pfizer's market capitalization over pharmaceutical giant (and Pfizer competitor) Merck & Co. for the first time ever. Because of Viagra, Pfizer became the biggest pharmaceutical company in the world. And in May 1998, the Dow Jones Online news reported that impotent men weren't the only ones getting a boost from Viagra. Reportedly, Bradley Pharmaceuticals, a company independent of Pfizer, predicted that because of Viagra, and the corresponding increase in sex among middle-aged consumers, sales of Bradley's vaginal lubricant insert Lubrin would skyrocket.

Despite its rosy beginnings, the good news surrounding Viagra began to shrink not long thereafter. In the summer of 1998, the lawsuits began. The first Viagra plaintiff was Diego Padro, a 63-year-old New Yorker, who claimed that Viagra caused him to have a heart attack. The most interesting claim in a lawsuit was that of Joseph Moran, a car dealer from New Jersey, who claimed that he crashed his car into two parked cars after Viagra "caused him to see blue lightning coming from his fingertips, at which point he blacked out."

Despite the problems borne by success, Viagra turned out to be one of the most revolutionary, innovative, useful drugs in history, and this was not lost on anyone. Shortly after Viagra was introduced, three Viagra researchers (Pfizer says hundreds were actually involved in the development of the drug), including Dr. Louis Ignarro of UCLA, were awarded the Nobel Prize in physiology and medicine.

When it comes to the body, people are often skeptical of new products. While there is little at risk in trying out a new office product or some consumer-electronic gadget, what you put in your body can often have a dramatic effect. Yet doctors continue to be some of the biggest innovators. That is one reason why medical advances in the past 100 years have been so remarkable. If it weren't for doctors pushing the envelope, we wouldn't be as healthy or live as long. But that doesn't mean that it is easy to get people to try something completely new, especially if it involves insertion into the body.

Educating a Nation
The Difficult Task of Bringing Tampax to Market

In 1929, Dr. Earle Cleveland Haas attempted to invent a product that could be manufactured and marketed expressly for absorbing a woman's menstrual flow. A general practitioner, Haas spent much of his spare time developing the tampon, and with good reason: At that time, there were no commercially available tampons on the market. In fact, the use of a tampon was almost unheard of. Rather, most women used absorbent external pads made of cloth. Because these traditionally had been laundered for reuse, disposable external pads were introduced commercially in the late 1800s.

In light of this fact, it was quite surprising that disposable, commercial tampons were not yet available in the twentieth century, especially because the idea had been around for ages. The ancient Egyptians fashioned disposable tampons from softened papyrus, and the Greek physician Hippocrates, writing in the fifth century B.C., described a type of tampon made of lint wrapped around lightweight wood. In Rome, women used wool, in Japan, they used paper, and in Africa, leaves of grass. Dr. Haas's inspiration came not from knowledge of the homemade tampons used by women since antiquity, but from observing the discomfort of his own wife and his female patients who had no choice but to wear bulky external pads.

It was during a visit to California that the good doctor happened on a modern solution. A friend there told Haas that she inserted a small sponge during that time of the month to absorb her menstrual flow. With that insight, Haas went back to his basement workshop in Denver and began to experiment. He took a long strip of cotton fibers about 2 inches wide and 6 inches long, and sewed it together. To compress this cotton even further, he invented a pliers-like device that could shape and squeeze the pad. And to enable a woman to remove the tampon without touching it, he attached a cord to one end. Dr. Haas also wanted to be sure that each new tampon was clean before it was inserted, so he decided that a woman had to be able to insert it without touching it. With inspiration from a telescoping paper tube he saw on his shelf, he created a device with two tubes in which one tube was slightly larger than the other to hold the tampon while the smaller tube would push the tampon into place. This apparatus was also easily disposable after use.

Dr. Haas knew that he was on to something, and was doubly cautious, afraid that if he explained his idea too carefully in his patent application, someone might steal his idea. In his application, dated November 19, 1931, he described his invention as "a catamenial device." The word *catamenial* is derived from Greek, meaning monthly. Nowhere in the application did he actually mention the word *tampon.*

A patent is not the only type of legal protection available for one's intellectual property, and Dr. Haas knew that, too. Understanding that he needed a unique name to go with his unique product, Dr. Haas set about to coin a name for his cotton tampons. He says that he came up with the brand name Tampax by combining the words *tampon* and *vaginal pack.* And to protect that name, he registered this trademark. Like obtaining a patent, registering a trademark is a way to legally protect intellectual property. A trademark is a unique word or symbol that distinguishes a business from its competition. The Nike "swoosh" is a trademarked symbol. Similarly, distinctive words, like Tampax or Big Mac, can be trademarked, and thus protected from imitators. (Copyrights, the other formal method of legal protection for intellectual property, relate to the written word. This book, for example, is copyrighted. Most inventors usually do not need a copyright.)

Armed with a product he knew half of the world's population needed, and legally protected with a patent and trademark, Dr. Hass needed some partners to get his product to market. His search landed him on the doorstep of Gertrude Tenderich, a woman that intuitively understood the value of Haas's invention. She also headed a group of investors that offered to buy Dr. Haas's patents and trademark outright. Haas accepted, and the Tampax Sales Corporation was chartered on January 2, 1934, with Tenderich as the president.

As there was no machinery yet devised to make the tampons, the president herself worked from home producing the new company's product, using a sewing machine and Haas's hand-operated compressor. She then hired some salesmen and set out to persuade drugstores in Colorado and Wyoming to stock tampons. The Tampax team immediately discovered the difficulty of introducing a product that is unfamiliar to people. If you had never seen an airplane before, you might be a little hesitant to fly in one, and if you had never used a tampon before, you might be even more hesitant about inserting one into your body. The fact that the product dealt with such an intimate issue at a time when such issues were kept private made the selling of the first tampons a very difficult endeavor. Some druggists feared that displaying the blue and white Tampax cartons on their shelves would offend their customers, and insisted on hiding them behind the counter. Others refused to stock tampons at all. And most newspapers refused to accept the advertising Tenderich hoped would generate demand.

It was a difficult job, going store by store, trying to sell and inform at the same time, but slowly, Tenderich and her associates wore down some of the resistance. One of their breakthroughs came when the *Denver Post,* the *Journal of the American Medical Association,* and some other publications agreed to accept Tampax advertising, if it included an address to which women could write for more information. Tenderich also understood that much of their success would depend on educating women about tampons and how they worked, thereby eradicating safety and hygiene concerns. So she launched an innovative ad hoc educational campaign whereby registered nurses were commissioned to give public lectures on menstruation and tampons. Squads of women were hired and trained to go door to door through residential neighborhoods to talk with housewives about the product. Sales picked up.

But still, Tampax was mostly a regional phenomenon. To expand the product and the business, Tampax would need much more capital than sales were able to raise around Denver. A partial solution came in 1934 when, for $25,000 plus royalties, Robert A. McInnes bought the rights to manufacture and sell Tampax tampons in Canada and the rest of the British Empire. By 1935, Tampax had sales of about $60,000; an improvement over the previous year but not enough to finance the nationwide marketing and education campaign needed to make Tampax truly profitable. So Tenderich headed east in search of someone who could help. A few days after her arrival in New York, Tenderich called her daughter and said that she had "found somebody who is really going to make a go of it. His name is Ellery Mann."

Like almost every other Depression-era innovator in this book, Ellery Mann was mostly out of work. When he did work, it was part-time, most recently, as the head of a trade magazine, *Drug Store Retailing.* As fate would have it, Mann's main mission was to find a new product to peddle, and when he met Gertrude Tenderich, he was in the midst of calling his contacts in drug companies to get tips about any hot new products coming on the market. This was a match made in an entrepreneur's heaven. Tenderich had the product Mann was looking for, and Mann was the promoter Tenderich needed.

A deal was struck. Under the agreement, Mann would organize a new company, Tampax Incorporated, to manufacture and market Tampax tampons. Tampax Incorporated was formally chartered in 1936. The first executive recruit was Thomas F. Casey, the choice for vice president and treasurer. Mann's other executive recruit was Earle A. Griswold, whom he hired as vice president in charge of manufacturing. Mann, Casey, and Griswold would guide Tampax for the next two decades. The three men were betting their reputations and careers on the hope that they could change the personal habits of millions of American women who had never even heard of a tampon.

Mann's marketing plan took aim at three different audiences: physicians, drug companies, and consumers. Mann believed that without sufficient advertising, the product and his company was doomed to fail, so he created an advertising campaign to attract all three of his target audiences. In trade magazines such as *Drug Store Retailing*, he emphasized the profit potential inherent in stocking and promoting his new product. Ads in the *AMA Journal* and various nursing magazines were educational in nature, focusing on anatomical drawings and technical descriptions of the tampon. These ads sought to educate professionals who were in a position to advise women about the product. The most important ads were those directed at the consumer. Using national magazines as his vehicle, Mann ran the first national Tampax ad on Sunday, July 26, 1936, in the *American Weekly*. This Sunday supplement was inserted in many major newspapers, and claimed some 11 million readers. The ad reflected the precarious nature of this high-wire act. Advertising such a sensitive topic to a national audience required a combination of aggressive selling and good taste.

Earle Griswold geared up to build production lines around a bank of sewing machines and five new compressors that incorporated improvements on the design of the old Denver machine. The work still required considerable hand labor, from cutting cotton at the beginning of the line to sealing the finished tampon in a cellophane wrapper. To perform all of these tasks, Griswold hired women at 28 cents an hour and purchased surgical quality cotton for the tampons.

Mann was optimistic. "Management is fully confident that Tampax will become a product enjoying a wide and profitable sale," he wrote, "but it must be realized that the use of the product represents a new departure in feminine hygiene and the factor of time necessary to educate women must be taken into consideration." The truth of this statement was seen in March 1937, when the company experienced what is still internally known as "Black St.

Patrick's Day"—returns from wholesalers exceeded outgoing shipments.

Despite this setback, Tampax had what other companies dream about: A patented, necessary item and a wide-open market. During the second half of 1937, sales doubled those of the same period in 1936, and sales for the year exceeded $500,000. Though the company still lost money, Tom Casey's numbers showed a profit of $39,000 for the second half of 1937. Mann reported to stockholders, "Tampax is destined to be a substantial success."

On the education front, Tampax hired its first full-time educational consultant, a woman named Mabel Mathews. In March 1941, Mathews established the company's first formal educational department. She began hiring and training consultants, "Tampax ladies" as they were known, all of whom had a professional medical background so as to command respect. The Tampax ladies visited colleges and schools, as well as trade shows and conventions. Their aim was to dispel myths and misconceptions about menstruation and sanitary protection. It was not always an easy task. To illustrate the difficulties, Mathews later recalled the time she gave a talk to a women's college in Virginia where Ellery Mann's older daughter was a student. After the talk, one of the young women announced to Mathews, "Marian Mann goes to school here and her father makes Tampax and she told me she wouldn't be caught dead with them."

As part of its education effort, Tampax had already begun to work closely with various researchers in order to test, and hopefully prove, the safety of this new product. A 1943 study by the Jefferson Davis Hospital in Houston found that, over a five-year period, women who used tampons were normal in physiology and menstrual function. (And in a sign of the times, the study also concluded that unmarried women had no difficulty using tampons.) Perhaps the most persuasive medical report of all was published in 1945 in the *Journal of the American Medical Association* by Dr. Robert Latou Dickinson. Dickinson's report was so favorable that it amounted to a virtual endorsement of tampons over external pads.

There comes a point in the life of a product where it either takes off or dies. Because Tampax had decided to fight both the educational and advertising fronts at once, by the time the United States entered World War II, the product had taken off. In 1942, Tampax tampons were available in 100 countries. But more than anything else, it was the war that turned Tampax tampons from a great new product into a household word.

The war catapulted tens of thousands of young women out of the kitchen and into military uniform. Millions of other women went to work in factories where they took over traditional male pursuits. Overnight, women had become busier and far more active; the kind of women Tampax long had targeted in its advertising campaigns. But now, instead of showing women swimming or dancing in magazine ads, Tampax ads showed women welding and marching. The posters in the drugstore display portrayed a woman in uniform with the slogan, "No time for a time-out."

Sales soared beyond Ellery Mann's most optimistic dreams. Tampons began to sell faster than Tampax could make them. In March 1946, the company marked its tenth anniversary. In his report to stockholders, Mann wrote, "We feel that we can point with pardonable pride to the fact that Tampax has in that period become one of the best-known names in the field of intimate feminine hygiene."

In 1984, the company changed its name to Tambrands Inc., and still manufactures and sells Tampax tampons in over 150 countries to more than 100 million women. In 1986, the editors of *Consumer Reports* magazine surveyed more than 100,000 products and services introduced in the previous half-century in order to select those that had exerted the greatest impact on everyday living. Among other familiar products such as air conditioners and running shoes, the editors chose the tampon as one of "50 small wonders and big deals that revolutionized the lives of consumers."

One thing tampons had in their favor was that team Tampax knew the potential it had with this product. The company knew the product was good, knew that women needed it, and knew that no one else had it. While none of these things made the introduction of Tampax's unconventional product any easier, Ellery Mann and company were likely solaced by the fact that they had something both very unique and quite necessary. A different problem altogether results when a radically new substance is created, people know that it's amazing, but no one knows what to do with it. This happens more than you may think. When it does, an innovative marketer is needed to turn it into a great product.

From a Cocktail Party to the Moon
Silly Putty's Wild Ride

As World War II got underway, Japan began to attack its Asian neighbors. Many of these were large rubber-producing countries that the United States depended on as trading partners. The dwindling supply of rubber, combined with America's massive effort to retool its military in the years that followed the attack on Pearl Harbor, led to an increasing difficulty as the United States tried to produce necessary goods made from rubber, especially truck and airplane tires, boots, and gas masks. The American War Productions Board put out a call to American industries to create a substitute for rubber.

In 1943, General Electric (GE) assigned one of its engineers, James Wright, to work on development of a chemically synthetic, all-purpose rubber alternative. Wright experimented with several combinations before combining boric acid and silicone oil. The two compounds solidified into a gummy goop inside his test tube. Wright accidentally dropped some of the substance on the ground and found that it bounced. He soon noticed other strange properties in the stuff he began to call "gupp." The new substance stretched farther than rubber, had a 25 percent greater rebound ability when bounced against a hard surface, and was able to withstand molds and decay, as well as a wide range of temperature extremes, all without decomposing. Even more curiously, the substance exhibited what is called an inverse thixotropy. Because it was a polymer with a unique molecular makeup, pressure applied to the polymer molecules slowly, by stretching the gupp for example, would deform the polymers, allowing them to take on a new shape. If you applied the pressure or force too quickly, the polymers snapped altogether. Curious indeed.

Despite its peculiar attributes, the substance was not an alternative to rubber. Though the gupp was interesting, it was soon considered an in-house oddity at the labs of General Electric. Yet it wouldn't languish for long; gupp was too unique a material to ignore. GE tried to find a commercial or industrial use for the stuff, but preoccupied by war and with no ready solutions available, its engineers were stumped. By 1945, with the war winding down, GE decided to send samples of gupp to scientists and engineers around the world, hoping to find a practical use for it. But none of them, including those on the U.S. War Production Board, found any use for the goo.

The substance became an oddity with no known usefulness, yet no one wanted to throw it away. It wasn't until six years after it was invented that someone finally came up with a use for the stuff. The year was 1949, the place, Boston. There, a Harvard physicist who had been sent some of the stuff brought it out on a lark to show his guests at a cocktail party he was hosting. A clump of the bizarre compound was passed around among the guests. Peter Hodgson, an ex-copywriter in dire financial straights, was one of the people who happened to be attending the party. Hodgson pointed out to another guest, a toy store owner named Ruth Fallgatter, how such a simple object seemed to keep the group of adults amused for hours.

Hodgson suggested to Fallgatter that they buy some of the stuff and sell it as a toy in her Christmas catalogue. Considering that no one had ever come up with a use for the stuff, this was not such a silly idea. Although Hodgson was already $12,000 in debt, he borrowed another $147, and bought 21 pounds of the stuff from GE. He and Fallgatter then put the bouncing, stretchy, snappy goop in clear compacts priced at $2 each, and waited.

Gupp outsold everything in Fallgatter's toy catalogue. Hodgson was sure that they had a winner, but Fallgatter disagreed, despite the robust sales. Peter Hodgson decided to market the stuff on his own. With his share of the profits, he hired a few Yale students and, along with his own three kids, they separated the putty into half-ounce balls and inserted them into colored, pull-apart plastic eggs. After rejecting 15 different names, Hodgson finally decided to call the stuff Silly Putty.

In February 1950, Hodgson took his creation to the New York Toy Show. Every single person he spoke with there, every consultant and advisor, told Hodgson to give up on the idea. But he was persistent, as driven innovators are wont to be, and eventually sold a few eggs to two big stores. Neiman Marcus and Doubleday Bookshops were the first stores ever to stock Silly Putty. At the same time, more convinced of its success than ever, Hodgson moved the Silly

Putty operation out of his house and into a barn in Connecticut. Needing packaging to ship his "eggs" in, he contracted with the Connecticut Cooperative Poultry Association for their excess egg cartons, which he thereafter used to ship his product.

In August 1950, only a few months after Hodgson started his operations, and just about a year after Ruth Fallgatter decided that she wanted nothing to do with this silly business, a writer for the *New Yorker* stumbled upon an egg of Silly Putty at a Doubleday Bookstore in Manhattan. Smitten, he wrote a glowing review of it in the "Talk of the Town" section. Peter Hodgson never had to worry about money again. He received 250,000 orders in 3 days.

The flood of orders continued, pretty much unabated, and by 1951, Hodgson was receiving more orders than he could keep up with. With the Korean War breaking out, however, the United States decided to ration silicone—the ingredient that put the silly in Silly Putty. This put Hodgson in a very precarious position. The publicity he received, and the ensuing deluge of orders that followed, is a strike of business lightning that rarely happens twice. Struck by lightning and hustling to fill back orders, Hodgson had to ration what little putty he had left without angering his new clients. It was a high-wire act, but he made it to the other side without falling.

By 1955, with silicone production back to normal, Silly Putty made a remarkable transformation. What began as a parent's play toy had evolved into a toy for children. Hodgson knew that as an adult plaything, Silly Putty was subject to the whims of culture. Today's Pet Rock is often tomorrow's basement bargain. Determined not to let this happen to his innovation, Hodgson decided in the early 1950s that the future of Silly Putty was with children, and he set about to make it a must-have child's toy. He did so in a way as innovative as his initial inspiration—he advertised on television.

At the time, television was a new medium, and the power of television advertising was not yet understood. This is even truer of children's advertising, then an unknown entity. But Peter Hodgson changed all that. Simple commercials touting the amazing properties of Silly Putty ("it bounces, it stretches, it picks up pictures from the newspaper!") were soon seen regularly on the *Howdy Doody Show* and *Captain Kangaroo.* By being one of the first advertisers ever on a children's show, Silly Putty helped sear itself into American consciousness. By the end of the decade, 80 percent of all Silly Putty purchases was for children. Says Peter Hodgson, Jr., "Successfully marketing Silly Putty as a toy resulted from my father's intuitive grasp of the silly relations occurring among the product's unique properties and the universal human experience." He adds, "It was a thinking kid's toy, and it has maintained its fascination, precisely because it doesn't fit in any category."

The 1960s was an amazing decade for Silly Putty. In 1961, the United States held its first Plastics Expo in the Soviet Union. There, next to plastic tubs and synthetic trays, was a display of Silly Putty. Soviet citizens were so enthralled by the amazing substance, so enamored of it, that they stood ten-deep trying to get a glimpse of the goo. Silly Putty was the undisputed hit of the show, so much so that the Soviet government soon recommended that tourists visiting the USSR should bring some of the stuff as a gift to Soviet citizens. Says Peter Hodgson, Jr., "Ordinary people have difficulty making sense of Silly Putty, which accounts for their fascination when they experience it." Hodgson, Jr., now a retired professor of Russian Literature from UCLA, was instrumental in stretching the toy into universality, when he introduced Silly Putty to Europe and the Soviet Union in the early 1960s. The apex for Silly Putty, literally, came in 1968 when Apollo 8 astronauts brought Silly Putty to the moon in sterling silver eggs, reportedly to alleviate boredom and to help fasten down tools in zero gravity.

While no one knew what to do with the goo when it was first invented, today, many more uses have been found for the putty. Silly Putty is touted as a grip enhancer, used by athletes to increase hand strength. Many therapists recommend squeezing it as a stress reliever. It can be used to clean computer keyboards, plug leaks, steady a wobbly table, and lift dirt from car seats and clothes. And, of course, nothing picks up stray pieces of Silly Putty better than Silly Putty.

In 1977, the product and Hodgson's company was bought by Binney & Smith (maker of Crayola Crayons). The formula and manufacturing process have remained essentially unchanged for 50 years, though in 1990, four fluorescent colors hit the shelves. In 1991, glow-in-the-dark putty arrived on the toy scene, and in 2000, 50th-anniversary gold putty was offered for sale. Yet classic Silly Putty is still the best-selling putty of all. According to Binney & Smith, a resurgence of interest pushed annual sales of Silly Putty to 2 million eggs per year in 1987, and today, it's closer to 6 million eggs, or about 90 tons, per year. To date, more than 300 million eggs (5,000 tons) of Silly Putty have been sold, enough to build a life-size replica of the Goodyear Blimp.

Silly Putty is now such an American institution that it has become part of the collection at the Smithsonian Institution's National Museum of American History. There, a vintage blue-and-yellow egg from the early 1950s is on display in the museum's "Material World" exhibition devoted to significant inventions and materials that have shaped American culture. "The Silly Putty collection tells many fascinating stories about how this unusual product became an American phenomenon," says John A. Fleckner, chief archivist at the museum. "We are interested in this collection because Silly Putty is a case study of invention, business and entrepreneurship, and longevity."

In 1976, the once-indebted Peter Hodgson died, leaving an estate of $140 million.

The Innovation Rules

- The radical idea is often met with scorn, and the innovator must meet that with patience and education.
- Nothing beats good publicity for increasing acceptance of an innovative product.
- Innovators must use patents, trademarks, and copyrights to protect their products.

!!!!!!!!!!!!!!!!!!!!!!!!!

If You Build It, They Will Come

A fundamental precept of business is that to succeed, a company must fulfill a market need. You have to give the customer what it wants, when it wants it, and do so in a way that is affordable while still being profitable. It is no easy task. Without tapping into a willing market and filling it with a product that solves some sort of consumer need, even the best, smartest, most cutting-edge business will fail. Conversely, the company that meets that demand best will thrive. It should be no surprise then that the market is a demanding taskmaster: If you do not do what it wants, you will be left behind.

Accordingly, market demand drives our economy, and not surprisingly, innovation, too. At least, that's how the theory goes. What is so interesting and amazing about the businesses and products in this chapter is that they turned the fundamental precept of our entire economic system on its head and succeeded outrageously anyway. Rather than demand creating supply, the innovations here were invented before a demand was even present. Supply created demand. Even though consumers did not know that they wanted these products, these pioneers created them anyway.

The lesson for the business innovator is that a lack of a ready market need not be an obstacle to a great idea. While it is far more ideal to find an unmet market need and meet it with an innovative product, these innovations prove that a truly great idea can find a market, even if you have to create one out of thin air.

Divine Intervention
The Inspiration for Post-it Notes

The Minnesota Mining and Manufacturing company, better known by its moniker 3M, is a company that truly values innovation. Its well-known brands include Scotchgard fabric protectors, Scotch-Brite scouring products, and Scotch tapes. The company operates in more than 60 countries and makes more than 50,000 products. 3M's corporate culture fosters creativity and gives employees the freedom to take risks and try new ideas. Founded in 1902, the company invented sandpaper in 1904, masking tape in 1925, transparent tape in 1930, electrical tape in 1945, surgical drape in 1950, fabric protector in 1956, synthetic running tracks in 1963, and so on. So when someone at 3M says they invented something new, people listen.

In 1968, 3M research scientist Dr. Spencer Silver said that he had invented something new. He was looking for ways to improve the acrylate adhesives that 3M used in many of its tapes, and in one of his experiments, Silver came upon an adhesive that didn't really stick to anything, but remained sticky even after it was repeatedly repositioned. The adhesive he had inadvertently created formed itself into tiny spheres, each with the diameter of a paper fiber. The spheres would not dissolve, could not be melted, and were very sticky individually. But because they made only intermittent contact to the paper they were applied to, they did not stick strongly when coated onto tape backings.

Silver knew that he had invented a highly unusual new adhesive, but the question was what to do with it. A glue that didn't stick very well might have been considered a failure at other companies, but at 3M it was more of a novelty, something to explore. Yet try as he might, Dr. Silver could not figure out what to do with his funny glue. He spoke with colleagues about the adhesive and they too were stumped. Silver was convinced that he had invented something special and refused to simply let it fade away. So committed was he to his innovation that for the next several years, Silver gave seminars to his colleagues at 3M, extolling the virtues of this new adhesive and showing samples of it in a variety of forms; in a spray can and as a bulletin board were the two used most prominently. Despite all this exploration, no one at the giant company could find a good use for the adhesive.

Getting a new product on the corporate agenda is not an easy task. Given that a business will have to expend untold amounts of money and effort into any new product launch, it is often necessary that the corporate innovator play politics and assemble a team of likeminded individuals who are behind the product. Without a committed team, even the most innovative products can die. So, in 1973, when Geoff Nicholson was appointed 3M's new products development manager for the commercial tape division, Spencer Silver knew that if his adhesive was going to ever find a home, he better get his new boss on board. Two days after Nicholson began his new job, Silver was in his office giving him a presentation. Convinced, Nicholson became the brave champion of a product that no one seemed to need.

Silver continued with the presentations, proffering his potential product, and hoping to find someone in the company who could put the adhesive to good use. As fate would have it, one of the many employees who had attended one of Silver's seminars was a development researcher named Art Fry. Although he was intrigued by the nonadhesive adhesive, like everyone else at the company, he too was stumped for a practical use for the glue. That is, until the day he really needed a sticky piece of paper, proving that necessity is indeed the mother of invention. As Mr. Fry stood singing in his church choir, he became frustrated, and not for the first time, that the little pieces of paper he used to mark his place in his hymnal kept falling to the ground. If only he had some sort of sticky bookmark. And then it hit him, in what a 3M spokesman calls "a moment of pure 'Eureka!.'" Art Fry thought about that glue, that crazy glue that Spencer Silver kept talking about. Fry realized that Silver's adhesive could make quite a reliable bookmark.

One of the things that makes 3M unique is its policy of allowing technical employees to spend 15 percent of their time on products of their own choosing. Fry quickly began to use this time working on his new sticky bookmarks. Attaching Silver's adhesive to the back of some notepaper, Fry created some sample bookmarks. In a second instance of inspired serendipity, he attached the sticky bookmark to a report and wrote on it. He realized that he had not created a bookmark at all. According to Fry, it was after writing the note on one of his gummy bookmarks and attaching it to the report that he "came to the very exciting realization that [his] sticky bookmark was actually a new way to communicate and organize information." The gummy bookmark begat a sticky note.

With the backing of his superiors, and an actual use for the long-dormant adhesive, Silver and Fry were able to get the sticky notes on 3M's new product agenda, which entailed: getting a budget, creating prototypes, refining the product, and product testing. But, as with anything new, there are always naysayers. Skeptics within 3M said that the notes would pose considerable processing, measurement, and coating difficulties. Some thought that the product was unfeasible, or too expensive. Fry's response? "Really, that is great news! If it were easy, then anyone could do it. If it really is as tough as you say, then 3M is the company that can do it."

And he was right. By 1977, 3M had refined the product enough and had produced enough usable notes that it could begin to test them. Fry began by giving the notes to fellow 3M employees. To say that there was a completely nonexistent market, even within the company, for the sticky notes would not be an exaggeration. No one had ever used the yet unnamed sticky notes before. People in the company had no idea what to do with Fry's product. But Fry realized the product's potential and how it could be used. He started by giving the notes to secretaries and showing them how documents could be kept neat and clean by writing notes on the sticky paper. The notes made a secretary's job easier, and as a result, the secretaries began to endorse the product within the company, convincing their bosses of the value of the notes. In this way, Fry not only created the very first market for his revolutionary product, but he was also able to get the budget he needed for test marketing.

Once outside the company, 3M marketers encountered the same problem Fry had found inside the company—people didn't know what to make of the new notes, and moreover, few wanted to pay for a product that competed with cost-free scrap paper. The four-city test marketing of 3M's new "Press and Peel Notes" was a dismal failure. Scuttlebutt within the company was that the notes would never get the go-ahead; 3M seemed to have created a confusing product no one wanted. Yet 3M marketers were encouraged by the fact that within the company, the notes had become outrageously popular. Once people understood how to use the product, how to communicate in this new way, the sticky notes were in high demand.

The question was not whether the product was useful, but rather how the marketing team was going to get people to try the new product so they could see how useful it was. Taking a play out of Fry's notebook, two 3M marketers flew to one of the test cities and began to give the product away. Wherever they went they gave the notes away, and orders flooded in from people that actually used the product. Although the concept of a loss leader is nothing new (selling a product for less than your cost to create a demand), it had never been used in the office supply industry before; but 3M realized that the time was now.

In 1978, 3M marketers went to Boise, Idaho, for what has become known in company folklore as the "Boise Blitz." They saturated the office supply industry with free samples and found that an astonishing 90 percent of the consumers who tried the now renamed Post-it Notes said they would purchase the product. As a result, the product was finally green-lighted. In 1979, Post-its were introduced in the 11 western states. Post-its were such a success that some enterprising individuals even bought up the product and shipped it to cities where it was not yet available.

The result is, as they say, history. In 1981, one year after their introduction, Post-it Notes were named the company's "outstanding new product." In 1990, ten years after their introduction, Post-its were named one of the top consumer products of the decade. Today there are Post-it Flags, Post-it Easel Pads, Post-it Fax Notes—over 400 Post-it products in all. Now retired, Art Fry is amazed, but not surprised, by the success of his brainchild. His take on the many innovative products that have followed the original Post-it Note: "It is like having your children grow up and turn out to be happy and successful."

If the story of the Post-it Note is about a product that was technologically feasible but took years to find its practical application, the tale of how Kitty Litter changed the world might be the exact opposite. It was created in an instant for an exact purpose. Yet, while their creation differs, what these products share is a market that didn't know it needed the product.

Here Kitty, Kitty, Kitty
Creating a Demand for Kitty Litter

Life after World War II was quite different than the years that immediately preceded it. From 1932, at the dawn of the Great Depression, until America's entry into the war at the end of 1941, American consumers had little of what is commonly now called "disposable income." Things weren't much different during the war years as citizens had to ration everything from gasoline to nylons to food. It wasn't until the late 1940s that Americans were able to live something resembling a normal life for the first time in a generation

One of the things that changed was that luxuries were finally affordable again. Among the things that people enjoyed after the war for the first time in many years was the company of a pet. At that time, there was no pet-care industry. No nutritious dog or cat food, no toys or pet superstores, nothing. Owners of indoor cats used everything from sand to ash to sawdust in their litter boxes, none of which worked all that well.

It is against this backdrop, in the middle of a cold Michigan winter in 1948, that a woman named Kay Draper ran into a problem: The sand pile that she used to fill her cat's litter box froze over. She decided to use the other common absorbent at the time, ash, but ended up with jet-black paw prints all over her house. Desperate for a solution, the good

Ms. Draper decided to visit her neighbors, the Lowes, who operated a coal, ice, and sawdust supply company across the way. She hoped that nice Mr. Lowe would have some sawdust she could use.

At the time, sawdust was also used as an industrial absorbent. But it was not perfect; if you spilled grease or oil on it, you had a major fire hazard. As a result, the Lowe factory had developed a new absorbent that it hoped to market—a kiln-dried clay dubbed "Fuller's Earth." Unfortunately, as an industrial absorbent, Fuller's Earth proved to be a hard sell and the company was stuck with tons of the stuff. Even their attempts to sell it to chicken farmers as nesting material had run afoul.

On a day that should be celebrated by cat lovers around the world, Ms. Draper asked 27-year-old Ed Lowe (who was working for his dad after his stint in the Navy) to help her. Rather than give her some sawdust, Ed, whose car's trunk was full of unsold Fuller's Earth, offered her some of that instead. Ms. Draper was not sure that clay was what she wanted, but being a good salesman, Ed Lowe convinced Kay Draper that Fuller's Earth would make great cat litter. She returned soon thereafter for more of the clay granules, and sent her friends to the Lowes for some Fuller's Earth, too.

Ed had a hunch that he may be on to something big. He filled ten paper bags with the stuff, labeled them with a grease pencil, "Kitty Litter," and tried unsuccessfully to sell them at local pet stores. No one knew what it was and, as a result, no one wanted it. The initial five-pound bags, priced at 65 cents, stayed on the shelf.

Ed Lowe was facing a problem that many innovative entrepreneurs have had to overcome—he had a product that was so innovative that there was no known demand for it. This is actually true for all the innovations in this book; they couldn't be called innovative if they weren't radically new in some sense. Yet what distinguishes the success of the products found herein against the failures of other products that we have never heard of is that these innovators were able to find their market. They were persistent enough, committed enough, and hardheaded enough, to see their idea through, even when the marketplace wasn't ready. The lesson is this: The customer is not always right. Sometimes the customer is flat-out wrong; That's what Edward Lowe learned.

Faced with no obvious market for what he considered to be a great product, Ed told the local pet store owners to give the bags away. Although the young veteran probably didn't realize that he was employing the loss leader strategy, Lowe nevertheless was a natural entrepreneur. He had good instincts. Once customers saw how good the product was, they were willing to pay money for Kitty Litter.

Lowe had visions of creating something bigger than a regional phenomenon, so he hit the road. Ed traveled the country attending cat shows and visiting pet shops in an attempt to move the product. Ed was (literally) willing to do the dirty work necessary to create his brand, and he cleaned hundreds of cat boxes each day in exchange for a booth at cat shows where he could display his new product. Crossing the country, Ed continued to sell Kitty Litter from the back of his 1943 Chevy coupe. Although it took a long time and a lot of litter, cat owners all over America eventually fell in love with Lowe's product.

The hard part about being an innovator is the struggle to get people to understand what you are doing. The good news is that you will have no competition. Ed Lowe sure didn't. It's the first mover's advantage: If you get your idea to market first, and people like it, you can control your industry. Ed Lowe did, and today, Kitty Litter and Lowe's other brainstorm, Tidy Cat (the first litter to be sold in supermarkets), command approximately 55 percent of the market. What started out as useless unsold clay has turned into an estimated 2.5 billion pound, three-quarters of a billion dollar industry that even has its own Washington lobbyist.

In 1990, a private investment group purchased Edward Lowe's company for $200 million. Lowe used part of the proceeds of that sale to establish The Edward Lowe Foundation (www.Lowe.org). The foundation helps and teaches other entrepreneurs how to get ahead. Says Lowe, "My life has been a testimony to the credo of the entrepreneur. People like me who have lived the dream should share their knowledge with others, because if private sector business doesn't help, then the American entrepreneur won't survive."

Some companies have more resources than others. Ed Lowe was remarkable because he created not just a product, but an entire industry through the sheer force of his will and commitment. He was almost personally responsible for the creation of the cat litter market. Other companies take a different tack. Not content to leave the fruits of their labor and innovation to the whims of an unpredictable marketplace, these companies do everything they can to make sure that there is a market for their product. Large corporations can afford to do so because they have the resources necessary to roll out a product in such a huge way that success, if not guaranteed, is practically assured.

Take, for example, the Gillette Company. This is a business that knows its customers. It tests, measures, and rates products and preferences continually. When a French man or an American woman shaves, Gillette has a pretty good idea what razor will be used and why. The company's laser-like focus on the shaving marketplace, and its unrivaled ability to forecast what men and women will buy, translates into a 72 percent market share in the United States and Europe. This dominance is born of a constant pursuit of better shaving technologies, a willingness to invest whatever is needed to manufacture its products properly, and a tested marketing strategy that works. As a result, you can pretty much bet that Gillette will know how to find the market for any new innovation.

The Mach 3 Razor
**The Tall Task of Replacing the Best
a Man Can Get**

Some businesses stumble upon innovation, some have it thrust upon them, and others, like Gillette, happily foster it. Gillette is a company that is so innovative, so committed to innovation, that whenever it rolls out a new product, it simultaneously begins to develop the replacement product. At Gillette, there is no such concept as getting ahead of itself; new products go on the drawing board as much as a decade before they are introduced. And so it was that in May 1994, several months before Gillette first shipped its hugely successful Sensor Excel razor in the United States, that marketing plans were already under way for the product that would succeed the Sensor Excel, the Mach 3 razor. Like some other companies, Gillette plans for obsolescence, but it does so by promoting innovation, so that when it says a product is "new and improved," it really is.

Since 1901, when King Camp Gillette invented the safety razor, Gillette has built a corporate culture around finding better, more lucrative ways to remove unwanted hair from the body. In 1971, Gillette took the shaving world by storm when it introduced Trac II, the first twin-blade razor with two parallel blade edges housed in a single cartridge. It did so again in 1977, when it launched the Atra, the first razor with a pivoting head. In the same time period, Gillette also unveiled the Good News, the first twin-blade disposable razor. But by the mid-1980s, with disposable razors taking up an almost 50 percent of the market, Gillette executives realized that disposables were a dead-end strategy.

With disposables, the razor had become a fungible commodity, with the buying decision based solely on price and convenience—a strategy that was not Gillette's traditional business model. The company had been founded on selling quality merchandise, not inexpensive items. Gillette needed something different, a product upon which the brand and its market share could be renewed. So rather than compete on the existing disposable playing field, even though they continued to capture a good portion of that field, Gillette smartly decided to create an entirely new razor category—the shaving system.

In 1990, after ten years of research and development, Gillette introduced its Sensor twin-blade shaving system. As with Trac II and Atra, the blade cartridges were disposable. But this time, the blades mounted on springs that allowed the razor to adjust to the shape of a man's face. This resulted in a shave that was significantly better. Gillette's design not only produced markedly closer shaves but also brought the company out of the disposables morass and back into its previous leadership position.

But, as indicated, Gillette never rests on its laurels. If two blades could produce a close shave, what might three blades do? So as it introduced the Sensor, Gillette already had its scientists trying to figure out if they could, or even should, trump themselves. What it knew was that the two-bladed Sensor worked because as the razor moved over the skin it forced hairs up and out of the hair follicles. The hairs are cut by the forward blade and then, as they start to retract, are cut again by the second blade. What then would be the purpose of a third blade? For much of the 1990s, Gillette scientists at the company's research lab in Reading, England, studied metallurgy, skin, and hair to figure out if they could make a triple-bladed system work. The problem was that the third blade continuously resulted in nicks and cuts. Accordingly, adding a third blade was not only a technical challenge, but it carried with it the added burden of seeming redundant. "What you need when you go to the board and ask for $750 million in development money is a product that can't fail," says William J. Flynn, the business director of blades and razors at Gillette. "It has to be preferable to what the customer is currently using."

After years of research, computer design, human trials and lots of scrapes, the Gillette scientists finally figured out that by setting each blade at an oh-so-slightly different angle so that the trailing blade could get close to the skin without tearing it, a third blade, rather than being unnecessary, was actually an advantage. Code-named Manx after the three-legged Isle of Man coat of arms, the new blade was found to cut 40 percent more hair than the Sensor Excel with less friction, making shaving more comfortable. The product took seven years to develop.

Gillette acknowledges that product quality is the sine qua non—the core value proposition around which everything else in the company revolves. "If you have a significantly and demonstrably superior product or service, it really is quite meaningful," says Tamar Goodblatt, a marketing consultant based in Portland, Oregon. "What Gillette did was to develop a new technology that worked. The tougher task was to get people to try it." Indeed, many great innovations have slipped by the wayside, unnoticed and unrewarded, in the history of consumer products. Of all the challenges faced by Gillette in the introduction of its superior, and expensive, new shaving system, the biggest one might have been this: How would it get its customers to turn in their old shaving system, the one that it had repeatedly promised was "the best a man can get"? Would there even be a market for an upgraded, more expensive, potentially gimmicky-looking shaving system?

Gillette, ever mindful of this, had to give its customers a reason for trying the new product. For the Mach 3, the proposition for the consumer had to be compelling, succinct, and easily understood around the world. Like everything else in the Gillette development process, it was a painstaking endeavor. Indeed, the value statement took two years, countless meetings, and innumerable focus groups to draft. It had to speak to a wide cross section of shavers, from the serious system shaver to the disposables user, from the executive in England to the cabdriver in Cancun.

Having tested the product with thousands of men, Gillette knew what mattered. Shaving can be time-consuming, irritating, and unpleasant. Men around the world craved the same thing: a close, clean, comfortable shave without nicks and cuts. Most men, according to Mr. Flynn, take between 100 and 500 strokes each time they shave, often going over the same area again and again. So the new razor had to offer a closer, quicker, less irritating shave. Finally, a value proposition emerged: The Mach 3 offered "the closest shave ever in fewer strokes—with less irritation."

What sounds so simple and obvious now was an "aha!" revelation inside Gillette. With this statement, all marketing efforts would have a common foundation upon which to build. Gillette could not only woo its own Sensor Excel customers to move up, but also grab market share among disposables users. "If you don't put it into language that gives a promise of something better, people won't try it," Mr. Flynn said. "But if you can create an appeal that gets them to try the product, the product will sell itself." Would this be true, even with a higher price tag? "In our consumer-use test study, we asked questions about what they would pay," Mr. Flynn said. "As we increased the price, their preference actually improved. That was the first time we'd ever seen that happen." So Gillette was extremely aggressive in it's pricing for Mach 3. It was priced 35 percent higher than Sensor Excel. Gillette knew that it had a superior product and decided on a superior price.

Gillette's Mach 3 marketing group, code-named the 225 Task Force, worked for five full years in concert with research and development to produce and orchestrate the introduction of the new product. By mid-1996, under John Darman, vice president of business management for male shaving, the task force began finalizing plans for a global introduction. With Mach 3, Gillette had a distinct advantage: The company had done it before. Gillette's experience with both the Sensor and the Sensor Excel had created a template for the manufacture, marketing, and promotion of a shaving system. In fact, Sensor had been so successful that it set off a string of 32 straight profitable quarters at Gillette.

The four lessons Gillette learned from Sensor were clear: (1) Because the product would likely take off immediately, manufacturing had to make sure that it had the capacity to avoid shortages from the get-go. (2) To facilitate a smooth introduction, all packaging, point of sale, and other promotional and support material had to be the same, and had to be easily translated into 30 languages and geographies. (3) All marketing and advertising had to be based on a single campaign, with minor local adjustments and translations. (4) Pricing would require some flexibility, but Gillette knew the base-minimum price it needed, based on the expected number of blades per user per year.

A global launch must be carefully planned and orchestrated to be successful. In this case, the Mach 3 was completely introduced around the planet in less than a year. According to Mr. Flynn, "We wanted to accelerate sales and profit growth. A global launch is the means to do that." The faster the product is in the market globally, the faster existing Gillette customers will trade up to the new product, and the faster new users will be drawn from competitors. Such quick-strike thinking leads to better financial results, adds Ms. Goodblatt.

Thus, all packaging, point-of-sale displays, and support material for the Mach 3 were the same around the planet. By creating a single look and feel to the entire global campaign, the Mach 3 achieved a branded look almost instantaneously. It also stepped up its public relations efforts for Mach 3 and received ten times as many mentions in the media for the product rollout as it had for Sensor.

By 1999, Gillette declared victory. Mach 3 blew away the skeptics and became the type of whirlwind success that product developers and marketers dream about. In just six months, Mach 3 became the top-selling razor and blade in North America and Europe. In fact, said Mr. Flynn, it took Sensor two years to reach the sales level that Mach 3 achieved in six months. In the United States alone, Mach 3 razors outsold Sensor four to one compared to Sensor's first six months on the market, and outsold Sensor blades three to one.

If success can be planned, then Gillette did it, and they will do it again. It is a safe bet that even as Mach 3 was hitting the stores, the Mach 4, or the Mach Excel, or whatever it is that the company calls its next innovative razor, was well along in its development cycle, and just as surely, plans are certainly under way to ensure you will buy it.

Revolutionary products may miss their mark far more often then they find it. For every Gillette Mach 3 razor and 3M Post-it Note, there are scores of new products that you never heard of, or that you heard of but didn't care about. The very nature of the new is that it requires people to give up the old, and that can be uncomfortable. Finding people who are willing to change is the challenge for any business involved in innovation. And, while using traditional methods like advertising and promotions can work, sometimes the marketing team has to be as innovative as the design team if its product is ever to see the light of day. Radically innovative marketing techniques are sometimes required.

It's Party Time
The Remarkable Marketing of Tupperware

If you have ever been invited to buy or sell Herbalife, prepaid phone cards, Amway, or any one of a hundred other products through some multilevel home-based marketing system, you have Earl Tupper and Brownie Wise to thank. Tupper was the inventor of his namesake product Tupperware, and Wise was the woman he tapped to help him find a market for his invention. She did so with the Tupperware Party, a unique in-home demonstration that was the forerunner of today's multilevel marketing method.

Tupper was born near the turn of the century in Berlin, New Hampshire, of good Yankee stock, and was always an entrepreneur and inventor by nature. His parents owned a commercial nursery, and young Earl was continually frustrated by his parents' lack of entrepreneurial zeal. Discontented with his hand-to-mouth existence, Tupper committed himself at a young age to what would become a lifelong plan of self-discipline and self-improvement. He pledged that he would "keep on trying until recognized and until attainment of success." As part of his New England Protestant upbringing, self-determination became the driving force of his life. At age 16, he committed himself to a strict diet and exercise regimen, and throughout his 20s, he recorded daily his height, weight, exercise regimen, and diet. In 1932, with his interest in inventing coming to the fore, he signed up for a correspondence course in business and advertising. His philosophy might best be summed up when he wrote, "Destiny finds a successful future for every open-minded, thinking individual who earnestly gropes for his destined work."

In 1933, frustrated by his inability to secure permanent work in the advertising field during the Depression, Tupper resolved to develop himself "mentally, physically, and spiritually, and thus make worthwhile contacts." Throughout the 1930s, Tupper maintained invention notebooks to record the conception and development of each of his ideas. He foreshadowed his life's work (and gave good advice to any would-be innovator) when he wrote: "To invent useful and successful inventions, those with inventive minds should not be afraid to look far, far into the future and visualize the things that might be. Remember, the things which are so commonplace today would have been the ravings of a fanatic a few years ago."

Yet despite his Protestant work ethic and positive outlook, Tupper, like most Americans, spent much of the 1930s struggling to feed his family. Working from his modest New Hampshire farm, he managed to keep his entrepreneurial flame alive with a small tree surgeon practice while still employed in other part-time work. In 1937, he was hired as a designer for DuPont. Becoming intimately involved in the forefront of the emerging plastics revolution, Tupper was immersed in the techniques of plastic manufacturing and production. As a designer, he was charged with creating a variety of different products, mostly for women: garter hooks, knitting needles, egg peelers, tampon holders, corsets, compact mirrors, and flour sifters. Despite his innovative spirit, self-discipline, and entrepreneurial zeal, however, Earl Tupper didn't have a woman's touch. Women simply did not like his designs.

By 1939, Tupper had learned enough about plastics to confidently establish his own company, the Earl S. Tupper Company. As a result of lengthy experiments with raw polyethylene during World War II material shortages, Tupper invented a method of purifying the by-product of the oil refining process into a material that was durable, flexible, odorless, nontoxic, and lightweight. Tupper was fascinated by the plastic's toughness and durability, properties not found in the hard, rigid plastics used until that time. Even better, this plastic could be colored and molded into any shape. He dubbed the polyethylene material "Poly-T: Material of the Future" and began to experiment, making plastic containers. Because of its unique properties, Poly-T could be molded into almost any shape and Tupper discovered that he was able to make lids for these containers that were truly revolutionary by creating an airtight seal.

In 1947, the patent for his ingenious "Tupper seal" lids was granted. After spending the first 42 years of his life designing mostly worthless knickknacks and doodads, Earl Tupper had finally used his Yankee ingenuity and go-getiveness to create a product of real value, something needed by postwar America. "Tupper was the Thomas Edison of the plastics world," says Jillian Lewis, a New York–based materials expert and arts historian. "What he did was find a widespread domestic use for plastics."

The first Tupperware object was a 7-ounce, milky white kitchen container, called a "bell tumbler" because of its unique shape. Like the rest of the containers that would follow, this piece of Americana, with its Tupper-sealed, airtight lid, was said by Tupperware to be "vermin and insect proof . . . unspillable . . . the first and only such articles the housewife needs." Tupperware trumpeted its unique containers in advertising, explaining that these were no ordinary lids, they were, according to Tupperware, "Patented Seal Cover Combinations." Whatever they were, they were definitely unique. Not only were they stronger and more snug than their more pedestrian lid cousins, but these tops were actually able to expel air as they were closed, creating the famous "Tupperware burp."

In 1947, *House Beautiful* portrayed the Tupper Corporation's kitchen containers under the title "Fine Art for 39 cents." The article extolled the virtues of the new containers as part of a 50-page special devoted to "Plastic . . . A Way to a Better, More Carefree Life." By 1949, Tupper had coined the actual term *Tupperware,* and was not shy about extolling its virtues himself. "Let's not think of Tupperware as a passing fancy. Instead, think of it as having taken its rightful place with other fine table furnishings—silver, linen, china." Yet despite his paternal love, and a rash of media attention, Tupper was having a difficult time finding anyone to buy his new product; a far cry from the "Tupperization" of the United States that he envisioned. Despite retailing efforts that included exclusive contracts, premium packaging, mail order, and shelf space in department and hardware stores, consumers were not used to high-quality plastic products and did not understand how to apply Tupperware's unique seal. By 1950, Tupper had failed to penetrate the domestic market in any substantial way. Although he was disciplined and brilliant enough to create a new kitchen tool, Tupper still lacked a woman's touch. Franklin needed his Eleanor. Clyde needed a Bonnie. And Earl Tupper needed a Brownie Wise.

Wise was a middle-aged divorced, single mother in Detroit who, not unlike many people in the post-war era, supplemented her income through independent sales, or what was known then as direct selling. It was sort of like being an independent sales representative for several companies. Ms. Wise worked with an outfit called Stanley Home Products where she sold, among other things, Tupperware. In 1948, Wise had created "Patio Parties" as a vehicle to sell her Tupperware stock. She added other products, like lipsticks and bath salts, as gift incentives, and found that women enjoyed coming to the parties. She was soon grossing more than $100 a week in Tupperware sales, and began to recruit other women to do the same. Her sales of Tupperware were among the highest in the country and Tupper identified her as someone who could potentially turn around the company's lagging fortunes.

In 1951, Tupper called Wise and wanted to learn everything he could about her Patio Parties. A dynamic woman, Wise was able to convince Tupper that what she lacked in formal business training, she made up for in understanding housewives and regular consumers, and her sales were her proof. Convinced, Tupper made the unusual and bold decision to hire Wise as his vice president in charge of Tupperware's distribution and sales network. He also daringly decided to base Tupperware sales *totally* upon her Patio Party template. Sales would be in-home only. Tupper continued to run production and to engineer and design products for Tupperware, while Wise was now in charge of public relations, promotions, and sales. This was remarkable for several reasons, not the least of which was that in the 1950s, few women worked, let alone ran corporations.

Wise's plan was to create a nationwide platoon of self-employed, nonsalaried, women to run Patio Parties around the country. Dividing the nation into distinct territories, she recruited regional managers, branch managers, district managers, and so on down to wholesale dealers who would make a profit selling Tupperware through the party plan. In October 1951, *Opportunity* magazine featured a full-page ad that promised "quick money . . . just for attending parties!" In the way that only ads out of the 1950s did, the advertisement went on to say that "Tupperware is the herald of a new era in the life of the American housewife! . . . you need no special selling ability or experience to make money with Tupperware. It sells itself on sight."

Tupperware Parties began to spread across American suburbia and soon became much more than selling vehicles. Part coffee-klatch, part sales shtick, and part social hour, the Tupperware Party enabled women to mingle, make money, and learn sales, all without ever having to endure a cold call. Average party attendance was 12 guests, and a top host could make in excess of $500 a week, although a far more average take was about $25 per party. Some women used Tupperware as barter, paying each other in plastic bowls for three or four hours of child care. "I thought the last thing I'd like to do was sit with a whole load of other homemakers and talk recipes," says Mara Sydney, a longtime Tupperware dealer in the 1960s. "But I had a great time. I made some money, socialized, and made some great friends."

Suburban 1950s housing tracts lacked the gathering places and community events that were hallmarks of older, more urban neighborhoods. Men were absent during the day, and women, confined to their homes with children, felt the loss of adult companionship. Wise quickly built a multi-million-dollar company by creating self-esteem and human interaction in an isolated, postwar suburban world, and the Tupperware Party became a cultural phenomenon. At a time when families were displaced from their relatives and isolated from one another, Tupperware parties helped fill the void. In many ways, Tupperware Parties were a 1950s version of the longtime desire of women to meet in groups. The quilting circles of the founding mothers, conscious-ness-raising groups of the 1960s and 1970s, and the book and investment clubs of today are all part of this tradition.

By 1954, Tupperware had a network of 20,000 dealers, distributors, and managers and Brownie Wise became the first woman ever to grace the cover of *Business Week*. Today, there is a Tupperware Party every 2.2 seconds, although these days, about 85 percent of sales occur outside the United States. Why? Brownie Wise was so successful at finding her market that most Americans already own plenty of Tupperware.

Like many products that finally see the light of day, the advantages of Tupperware were self-evident. A far more thorny problem arises when an individual or business creates a great new product, but consumers can't see its advantages. This happens, for example, when the product is so unique that people don't know what to make of it, or when the advantages are actually invisible to the naked eye. In this case, finding a market is very difficult.

Brushing Up
Convincing America of the Benefits of Crest

The bristle brush, invented in China, did not become part of western society until the seventeenth century. Like toothbrushes, compounds for cleaning teeth (and freshening breath) had been used since ancient times. Early Egyptian, Chinese, Greek, and Roman writings describe numerous mixtures for both pastes and powders, including powdered fruit, burnt shells, talc, honey, ground shells, and dried flowers. Modern toothpastes began to appear in the 1800s. Chalk was popularized by John Harris in the 1850s, and Dr. Washington W. Sheffield, a Connecticut dentist, put his popular Dr. Sheffield's Creme Dentifrice, packaged in a collapsible tube, on the market in 1892. But with all these products, no one had ever found a way to reduce dental decay. By the start of World War II, dental disease had become one of the most prevalent health problems in the United States, second only to the common cold. It is estimated that over 700 million cavities were developed each year.

It wasn't that scientists didn't know what caused cavities. Researchers knew that carbohydrates in food were converted to acids by enzymes produced by bacteria in the mouth. These acids attack and dissolve tooth enamel leading to cavities. But what could be done about it? Some researchers aimed at killing or retarding the growth of bacteria. Others thought that it was the enzymes that had to be attacked. No one really knew for sure. The search for that magic solution was ever elusive.

But there was a clue. For years, children in several western towns were virtually without cavities. In 1939, a dentist named H. Trendley Dean, working for the U.S. Public Health Service, decided to study the anomaly. Dean examined water from 345 communities in Texas. He determined that what these communities had in common was the natural presence of fluoride in the water. Dean concluded that the fluoride corresponded to a lower incidence of dental cavities, and contributed to what he described as "beautiful white teeth." Scientists at Procter & Gamble (P&G), a company that had recently entered the toiletries business with its Prell shampoo and Gleem toothpaste, were able to duplicate this phenomenon in the lab, showing that tooth enamel became more resistant to acid when treated with fluoride. They then began work on finding a way to include a fluoride compound in toothpaste.

Initial results were not promising. It turned out that the ingredients that made up toothpaste at the time, abrasives for cleaning and binders that held the composition together, were incompatible with known fluoride composites. But given that a need creates a market, P&G was determined to fund and continue the research. Over 500 different fluoride compounds were tested before one finally showed some promise—stannous fluoride.

P&G was not alone in this research. While its white-coated scientists had toiled long and hard to identify the secret ingredient, a graduate dental student at Indiana University, Joseph Muhler, had also found that stannous fluoride could be the key to creating an effective tooth dentifrice (toothpaste). Muhler's published work came to the attention of P&G management, and in 1950, the company and Indiana University made an arrangement to have Muhler and his team work on the development of anti–tooth decay ingredients. Before long, Muhler's group had discovered the combination of ingredients necessary to make an effective anticavity toothpaste. A patent was issued to Indiana University under which P&G paid royalties for the exclusive right to use the fluoride compound.

Clinical trial began immediately. In 1951, 1,200 schoolchildren in Bloomington, Indiana, public schools became the first study group for a toothpaste that contained stannous fluoride. Among children aged 6 to 16, one test showed an average 49 percent reduction in cavities. Another test showed a 36 percent reduction. The study was later expanded to include a total of 4,500 children and adults, and all results were encouraging.

Crest with Fluori-stan was test marketed in three areas beginning in 1955, but initial sales were disappointing for two reasons. The first was the inertia often faced by any groundbreaking new product: It threatens the old guard, those who often have turf to protect. Said J. Roy Doty, the then-secretary of the4 Council on Dental Therapeutics, "We know of no present adequate demonstration that any dentifrice presently on the market is significantly useful in preventing tooth decay except as it assists the toothbrush in the prompt removal of sugar residues from the mouth." The then-secretary of the American Dental Association, Harold Hillenbrand, said "The American Dental Association is not aware of evidence adequate to demonstrate the claimed value of Crest. Evidence of the value of adding a fluoride in dentifrices is [not] convincing." Could it be that dentists had a vested interest in tooth decay?

The second reason that initial sales of Crest were so slow was more problematic. Consumers did not know what fluoride was or what it could do, and thus were skeptical of Crest's benefits. Moreover, P&G was in the unenviable spot of having to prove a negative: Because its claim was that users would have less cavities by using the product, consumers, never a patient bunch, would have to wait a year or two to see any benefits, and not many were willing to do that. The basic problem was that Crest's unique formulation could not be seen by consumers. What was needed was a way to convince them that the product performed as advertised. P&G decided that consumers needed to hear of the benefits from a believable authority.

The obvious candidate was the American Dental Association (ADA), despite what Mr. Hillenbrand had said. Beginning in 1954, P&G submitted to the ADA the results of the company's extensive clinical tests. The ADA had a system already in place for such a review. Its review panel appraised, evaluated, and when appropriate, recognized beneficial oral hygiene products, both as support for the dental profession and as a guide for consumers to help them sort through often exaggerated advertising claims. Because of Crest's claims, the ADA standing review committee cast an especially skeptical eye on toothpaste advertising. Indeed, the ADA had never formally "recognized" any toothpaste.

P&G also knew that it is the nature of dental care for patients to ask their dentist for advice regarding dental care. So while the ADA was reviewing P&G's claims of Crest's capabilities, the company also sent out teams around the country to explain to dentists firsthand the value of fluoridated toothpaste. Meeting with them at conferences and in their offices, the P&G "detailers" explained the scientifically proven value of the toothpaste.

After an extensive five-year review, the ADA committee submitted the findings to the ADA Council on Dental Therapeutics, its decision-making body. On August 1, 1960, the *Journal of the American Dental Association* reported "Crest has been shown to be an effective decay preventative dentifrice that can be of significant value." But that was not all; the ADA was so impressed with what it saw that it went a step further. For the first time in its history, the ADA granted the use of its name in consumer advertising for a commercial product.

Sales soared. Within a year, Crest's sales doubled. By the end of 1962, sales had tripled, and before long, Crest became the best-selling toothpaste in the United States. Pushed by the success of its innovative toothpaste, P&G grew rapidly. By 1985, it had become the largest manufacturer of over-the-counter drugs in the United States.

The Innovation Rules

- The attributes of a new product are not always obvious; it is sometimes necessary for the wise innovator to teach people how the product can benefit them.
- Knowing what people want, like, or need will enable you to innovate in a way people will respond to. Know your market.
- Know your limitations, and bring in others who can fill your gaps.

!!!!!!!!!!!!!!!!!!!!!!!!

Money, It's a Drag

While inspiration often happens in an instant, innovation can take years. Great ideas are not all that difficult to come by for the creative mind. But an idea is just that—an ephemeral thought. Da Vinci conceived a flying machine but never built an actual helicopter; it remained nothing more than a page in his notebook. In fact, it is not farfetched to say that the constraints of time and space inherent in physical reality that challenge any creative person are simple when compared to the extra burden of profit put upon the creative businessperson. A painter can get an idea for a painting and paint it. A composer can put the tune in his head to paper. But the inspired business innovator must consider not just time (how long it will take to get the product to market) and space (how to fashion the product), but profit as well (no explanation needed). Writing a catchy tune is easy compared to creating a profitable product.

Because profit is what business is all about, isn't it? If the problem with capitalism is that it fosters competition over cooperation, the beauty of it is that it rewards the mighty. To come up with a great idea that makes you a bundle is indeed a great reward. Profit is the challenge and the hope, the burden and the benefit. For the business innovator, a great idea can be a loser if it is so expensive to create, or the market is so specific, that it can't make money. Getting a return on your inspiration often requires finding the money and other resources necessary to make the product cheaply enough and in a great enough quantity that a profit is assured. Let's see Van Gogh try that!

Bottoms Up
Diapering a Nation with Pampers

In 1956, Procter & Gamble (P&G) researcher Victor Mills was asked to care for his newborn granddaughter. Delight turned to despair when he found himself having to change the baby's diaper. At the time, changing a diaper, never a pleasant task, was far more messy and labor-intensive than today because it involved laundering cloth diapers. But Mills, unlike most grandfathers, had a staff of able engineers ready and able to help him out. He assigned a group of P&G researchers the task of researching an idea that came to him in the middle of his unenviable chore. The question he posed was this: Is it possible to create a diaper that is absorbent and leak proof, that will keep babies dry, and, most importantly, is disposable?

This is not to say that there were no disposable diapers on the market at the time. In 1946, a Connecticut housewife named Marion Donovan invented the "Boater," a waterproof covering for cloth diapers. Boaters were made of parachute fabric into which a regular diaper was inserted. Ms. Donovan was granted four patents for her diaper designs, although none was a commercial success. Similarly, there was a high-priced Swedish import brand of disposables called Chux, which accounted for less than 1 percent of the billions of diaper changes in the United States each year. Chux were used mostly by traveling parents when cloth diapers could not be laundered. The problem with the imports was that they were far too expensive for daily use and mothers didn't think they were very good. P&G was aware that an almost limitless market was waiting to be tapped by the company that could revolutionize diapering: The baby boom was well underway, population levels were accelerating, and initial market research produced a favorable response to the possibility of an affordable disposable diaper. So P&G gave Mills the go-ahead to research his idea.

The initial plan was to develop a highly absorbent and pleated pad that would be inserted into a specially designed plastic panty. It took P&G only six months to create the prototype diaper and testing began almost immediately in Dallas. But with average temperatures hovering around 93 degrees, the plastic panty made babies uncomfortable, and the first American-made disposable diaper was a bust. The engineers went back to the proverbial drawing board and by mid-1959 had the first-ever "new and improved" disposable diaper ready for market.

The new diaper was softer and more absorbent, with an improved moisture barrier between the wet padding and the baby's skin to keep most of the moisture away from the child. The real problem P&G faced was not creating a product that would work, but creating a product that would be cost-effective. At the time, there were no machines or factories that were capable of attaching the exterior plastic lining to the middle padding to the top layer of absorbent material. Instead, 37,000 diapers were prepared by hand for the next market test in Rochester, New York. But despite the production difficulties, the results were very encouraging. Two-thirds of the parents who participated said that the product was as good as or better than cloth diapers.

Based on these results, P&G was compelled to allocate the resources necessary to mass-produce the diaper. But it wasn't easy. Says one engineer who helped design the system, "It was the most complex operation the company ever faced. There was no standard equipment. We had to design the entire production line from the ground up. It seemed a simple task to take three sheets of material—plastic back sheet, absorbent wadding, and water-repellant top sheet—fold them in a zigzag pattern and glue them together. But glue applicators dripped glue. The wadding generated dust. Together they formed sticky balls and smears, which fouled the equipment. The machinery could run only a few minutes before having to be shut down and cleaned." Procter & Gamble invested millions of dollars in its attempt to create a viable production facility.

Undeterred, the company pressed on, only to be faced with an equally vexing resource issue. The next market test came in December 1961 in Peoria, Illinois. The question was: With the new diapers on, would the babies play in Peoria? Again, the mothers liked the product, but the cost to produce the diapers meant they would be paying ten cents per diaper, and *that* didn't play in Peoria. If the company was going to make its huge investment pay off, it would have to find a way to lower the cost per unit. Again, after much testing, the marketing department at P&G concluded that the company would have to drop the price per diaper 40 percent for its financial commitment to the product to pay off. The only practical way to do that was to increase volume.

Says another P&G engineer, "Do you realize what that entailed? For each one cent retail price reduction, vast increases in volume would be needed." And with the production facility experiencing problems, this was not so easy to accomplish. Yet, the demographics remained compelling. If P&G could figure out how to produce the product cheaply enough, a nation of babies was waiting to be diapered. The company forged on, betting the bank on the fact that if they produced enough, and thereby lowered the price enough, they could revolutionize diapering. Now, only a name was needed. After experimenting with Tads, Solos, and Larks, P&G decided upon Pampers. Finally, with a price of six cents per diaper, and a huge financial gamble, Pampers went on sale August 30, 1961.

The product was so novel that many merchants didn't know where to display it. Initially, Pampers were found everywhere from the paper products aisle to the convenience food section, from drug stores to grocery stores and even department stores. But confusion soon gave way to convenience. The diapers finally showed up in the baby section of the supermarket and new mothers soon discovered Pampers. It wasn't long before disposable diapers became all the rage. By the late 1960s, the diaper pail and laundry truck were practically a memory.

Pampers was not only an innovative product, it created an entire new industry. Today, the disposable diaper market is a $4 billion a year business. In the United States, disposable diapers are used 95 percent of the time. In France, they are used in 98 out every 100 diaper changes. According to the *New York Times,* Victor Mills's innovation is "along with Bic pens and microwave ovens . . . a symbol of the culture of convenience that permeates most modern, time-pressed societies." New parents can thank the company that was willing to put its money where the tush was.

As Joel Grey said in *Cabaret:* "Money makes the world go 'round." That is truer in business than in any other field of human endeavor. Finding the money to bring your innovation to market is often *the most* critical element to the success of the venture. And when you find it, either through a corporate budget allocation or from outside sources, it usually has more than a few strings attached. When a venture capital firm agrees to give you $5 million, it may ask for some seats on your board, a say in the execution of your business plan, or some other possibly meddlesome demand. Five million dollars buys a lot of opinions. So being able to maintain control of your venture while still finding the money you need is no small feat. It's not quite as exciting as getting your idea to market, but it's not chopped liver either.

When you think about modern inventions, very few have had the impact of the Palm Pilot. Almost overnight, everyone seemingly went from carrying a bulky calendar organizer to using a slick handheld computer—that was able to zap information to other machines of its kind with infrared rays no less! The personal digital assistant (PDA) revolution was almost as remarkable as the desktop computer revolution; it changed how people work and live. So just how did Palm maintain control of its revolutionary product and get it to market without giving away the store? Good question.

The Third Time's a Charm
The Evolution of the Palm Pilot

Palm Computing Inc. shipped its very first Palm Pilot in April 1996. This cool tool fit into a shirt pocket, stored thousands of addresses and appointments, and was cheap enough to appeal to a mass market. Within a year and a half, Palm had shipped more than one million Palm Pilots, making it the fastest-selling consumer-electronics product ever. The brief inauspicious history of PDAs that preceded it makes this feat even more remarkable.

Apple spent $500 million on its ill-fated, much-derided Newton before bailing out of the PDA market altogether. Kleiner Perkins Caufield & Byers, the powerful Silicon Valley venture-capital firm, funded a startup called GO Corporation to pioneer the handheld market. GO spent $75 million before going belly-up. All told, startups and other companies spent more than $1 billion trying to crack the PDA market, all to no avail. It would be Jeff Hawkins and his colleagues at Palm Computing, spending only $3 million to develop a workable PDA, who would launch the real PDA revolution.

Why did they succeed where so many others had failed? The story of the Palm Pilot is the story of obsession, partnership, big mistakes, and sheer tenacity. The story begins and ends with Jeff Hawkins. Hawkins graduated from Cornell University in 1979 with a degree in electrical engineering. He went to work for Intel, but lasted just three years at the company. "I wanted more responsibility. Intel said I needed more seniority." So Hawkins took a job at GRiD Systems, a small Silicon Valley startup whose business goal was to design a computer that you could carry, a wild concept in the early 1980s. In 1986, Hawkins, who was becoming increasingly interested in how the brain functions, decided to enroll in UC Berkeley's graduate program in biophysics. Although he left Berkeley in 1988 without a Ph.D., he had an idea. His research into neural networks focused on how the human brain could recognize patterns. His previous work in Silicon Valley naturally lead him to extend this thinking to computers. Hawkins developed an algorithm for handwriting-recognition software. He called it "Palm-Print" and it has since shaped not only his life, but millions of lives.

Hawkins left Berkeley and joined GRiD again, this time as its vice president of research. He was charged with developing pen-based hardware and software to complement the PalmPrint software he had patented and then licensed to GRiD. In 1990, the company unveiled the GRiDPad, the world's first serious pen-based computer. But as often is the case with first generation inventions, the machine was slow, clunky, and ugly. Although his first attempt at a pen-based computer would prove to be strike one, the GRiDPad was nevertheless truly innovative, and innovation spawns imitation. Trade magazines loved the GRiDPad and a virtual gold rush ensued. An array of computer giants—such as IBM, NEC, and Samsung—announced their own plans to launch similar devices. Kleiner Perkins poured money into GO. And Apple, which had been working on its Newton since 1987, shifted into high gear.

"It was about then that I decided I didn't want to be at Tandy [who had recently purchased GRiD]," Hawkins says. "I knew what I wanted to do, and I was in a position to do it on my own." What he wanted to do was to start his own company. Palm Computing was born in January 1992. While Hawkins had an idea and a business, he lacked a plan, a product, financing, and partners. He did have a reputation, however. One of the first people Hawkins met with was venture capitalist Bruce Dunlevie. Dunlevie says that he knew right away that Hawkins was "someone who is able to synthesize where technology is today and then advance it. Someone who knows intuitively what people care about." Dunlevie's firm, Merrill, Pickard, Anderson & Eyre, wanted to be Palm's lead investor. Hawkins also talked with Sutter Hill Ventures, another prominent VC firm in Silicon Valley. He accepted $500,000 from each of them, and $300,000 from Tandy.

He did so without giving away the store. All too often, entrepreneurs are forced to barter away too much of their business in various rounds of VC funding. The danger is that by the time they get their product out there, they have become a minority owner of their own business. Hawkins avoided this trap because he was strong and had a killer application. But even with funding, he knew that he still needed a plan and a product. What he didn't know was that he also needed a partner.

Martha Stewart has a business partner named Sharon Patrick who runs much of Martha's media empire. Martha likes to compare Ms. Patrick to a sturdy Jeep—solid and dependable. Every entrepreneur needs a Jeep, and Jeff Hawkins found his in Donna Dubinsky. After they met, Ms. Dubinsky gave Hawkins a list of references. She also asked him for his. Each person she talked with said that Hawkins was brilliant, had integrity, and could use some help. Donna Dubinsky signed on with Palm Computing on June 15, 1992. She was the first executive Hawkins hired, and the most important person behind the Palm Pilot other than its inventors. "We have complementary skills, and that makes for a good relationship," says Hawkins. "We rarely disagree, and we can usually anticipate each other's actions. A year after Donna joined Palm, I wrote a review of her performance and surprised her with it over lunch. She had already done the same thing—she'd written a review of me! That's how in sync we are." He adds that their relationship "felt great from the start. She had no hidden agendas."

Dubinsky found Hawkins to be equally straightforward. "He said he needed someone who would respect him as a product guy," she says. "And I had never seen anything like what he was talking about—electronics in the palm of your hand. It was the first time in a long time that I'd been really jazzed."

Dubinsky knew that one of her first jobs was to create a business plan. She and Hawkins decided on several principles. First, Palm would not design any hardware, only software. Hardware would be left to partners. Second, the software would need to be powerful enough to rival desktop machines. Third, Palm's products would target individual consumers, not business users. And finally, Palm would focus on getting well-known partners.

It was a carefully crafted plan, but it was wrong and never worked for a variety of reasons. Casio agreed to manufacture the handheld device that would run Palm's software. Geoworks agreed to provide an operating system.

Intuit agreed to provide personal-finance software, and America Online came on board as well. "I'd come to a meeting, and there would be people from six different companies sitting around the table," Dubinsky recalls. Seemingly every detail had to be signed off by every partner. It was innovation by committee, and Palm's debut product reflected the problems with this approach.

The device, called Zoomer PDA, was priced at $700; far too steep for a mass-market consumer product. Moreover, Zoomer had a very small keyboard, and its PalmPrint handwriting-recognition software didn't work quite right. The device included drivers for printers and fax machines, making it bigger and slower, even though few users expected to print or fax from a PDA. Says Hawkins, "It was the slowest computer ever made by man. It was too big and too expensive. We executed badly." Strike two.

Palm survived this major gaffe for two reasons. First, it ran a lean ship. "I was intent on raising plenty of money and spending it as slowly as possible," says Dubinsky. "When I was at Apple, I saw how being 'overcapitalized' gave you the freedom to make mistakes." Second, Palm was lucky enough to be second to market (and luck has no small measure of importance when it comes to creating a breakthrough product). In its zeal to gain the first mover's advantage, Apple introduced its PDA, the infamous Newton, a mere two months before Zoomer hit the streets. Newton was a dog for many reasons, not the least of which was that it couldn't recognize handwriting—a big problem when it was being touted as the first PDA able to recognize handwriting. The nadir for Newton may have come when the comic strip *Doonesbury* spent a week deriding the poor thing, with gags such as having the character Mike write in "pick up dog at vet" and having Newton read it as "sick log is wet."

Because Zoomer arrived after Apple's pathetic first-generation PDA, it was spared all the ridicule heaped upon

Newton. Zoomer was fortunately lost in the Newton debacle, as were a host of similar products that followed. "The entire market was lousy," Dubinsky says. By the end of 1994, most companies either went out of business (GO liquidated by 1994) or stubbornly persisted (Apple introduced new versions of the Newton).

Palm took a different route. The company had misfired badly, but thanks to Dubinsky's frugality, it still had money on hand. During the spring of 1994, Palm conducted in-depth surveys of consumers who had purchased Zoomer. More than 90 percent of Zoomer owners also owned a PC, and more than half of them bought Zoomer because its software transferred data from Zoomer to their PC, and vice versa. Consumers weren't looking to replace their PCs, they simply wanted to complement them. They didn't want a PDA that would compete with their computer, they wanted one that would compete with their planner. Palm learned an important lesson in the process: Knowing who your customers are is one of the best ways to ensure that you will stay in business.

Palm's cumbersome team disintegrated and Hawkins took some time off. When he came back, says a Palm colleague, "he was like Moses holding the tablets." But this time, there were only two commandments. The first had to do with software. Hawkins, like so many of his competitors, had been trying to write code that would enable Zoomer to recognize individual handwriting. That meant the software had to be complex, leading Zoomer to be slow. Hawkins's first revelation was this: Instead of having Mohammed go to the mountain, he would bring the mountain to Mohammed. Instead of the PDA learning everyone's handwriting, everyone would have to learn the PDA's handwriting.

Said Hawkins, "People like learning. People can learn to work with tools. Computers are tools. People like to learn how to use things that work." This logic resulted in the famed "Graffiti"—the handwriting-recognition software that differentiated the Palm Pilot from every other device on the market. With Graffiti, each letter is made by writing in a uniform way. No individual handwriting allowed. The initial reaction was mixed, but mostly negative. "People were saying, 'Sure, we're going to ask people to learn a whole new way to write,'" one Palm insider recalls. But once they tried it, and found that learning Graffiti was actually a fairly easy process, most people thought that it was pretty darn cool.

The second commandment had to do with the device itself. It had to be small, simple, quick, and cheap. Which features were mandatory? Which could be sacrificed? Which could be optional? With each revision, the product kept getting smaller and cheaper. By August 1994, less than three months after Hawkins began rethinking the PDA, Palm had a mock-up of its new device. This product would fit in a shirt pocket, would run on AAA batteries, and its four core functions were a calendar, an address book, a to-do list, and a memo pad. It would cost less than $300, and unlike the first-generation GRiDPad, was simple and elegant. The product got a code name: Touchdown. The third time's a charm.

It's a great thing to learn from one's mistakes, but it is quite another to persuade investors that you can get it right the third time. So Jeff Hawkins, Donna Dubinsky, and their third musketeer, Ed Colligan, met again with their VC partner Bruce Dunlevie at Merrill Pickard. Dubinsky and Hawkins told Dunlevie that they finally had the right product. This time, they said, Palm should not be just a software company. The company really needed to design, build, and market the entire device itself if it was going to be done right. Dunlevie said, "You know how to do this, right?" Hawkins said he thought so. "Then do the whole product," Dunlevie told Hawkins. Hawkins was amazed. "I didn't think that doing the whole product—both the hardware and the software—was an option," he says. "It was expensive. I was a young guy. I had never thought about doing anything that big alone."

Encouraged, they carried on, knowing that the only way to succeed was to continue to run a tight ship. And so they did. In all of 1994, for example, the company hired only one new employee. Instead, Hawkins and Dubinsky assembled a team of design and manufacturing companies, and paid each with a little cash, lots of options, and the promise of glory. "We created a virtual company," Hawkins says. Their real challenge was figuring out how they were going to market the thing. Ed Colligan sums up the dilemma: "We had a killer product. But the market was a dog. And we had no money to fund a launch. What were we going to do?"

Dubinsky figured that Palm needed $5 million to bring Touchdown to the endzone. She wanted to get $2 million from a new corporate partner, $2 million from venture capitalists, and then leverage the rest. But most companies were far more interested in picking Palm's pockets than in forging a meaningful partnership. Dubinsky broke off negotiations time and again, as it became more and more apparent that potential partners didn't want Hawkins's intellect, they wanted his intellectual property.

In early 1995, as with so many startups, the money chase began to consume their time and energies. "We were in a tough spot," she says. "We were going to have to start spending money." Even optimistic Jeff Hawkins understood that the company was in a very bad position. If it ran out of money then all their efforts were for naught. Says Hawkins, "This was the one time when I knew we were at risk."

Dubinsky began looking for potential partners, hoping for even the most remote match. Then one name leapt off the page: U.S. Robotics. In less than five years, the modem maker had seen its revenues jump from $50 million to almost $1 billion. Dubinsky also knew that U.S. Robotics, based in Illinois, was looking for a foothold in Silicon Valley. She called a friend who arranged an introduction. Hawkins and Colligan met with Jon Zakin, then the vice president of business development for U.S. Robotics. Colligan watched Zakin as Hawkins demonstrated Touchdown. "It was wild," Colligan says. "He got it immediately, like a snap of the fingers. He told Jeff, 'You've thought this thing through.'" Zakin wanted in.

Dubinsky suggested that U.S. Robotics invest $5 million, and Zakin agreed to consider the offer. At a second meeting, Zakin was even more upbeat, but never mentioned the $5 million offer. That night, he called with a different offer: What if U.S. Robotics bought Palm Computing? "It was almost terrifying how decisive they were," Dubinsky says. "After all the frustrating negotiations we'd been through, these guys turned on a dime. They were ready to buck conventional wisdom."

It was a risk for everyone. For U.S. Robotics, the purchase could have been an expensive wild goose chase. For Palm, it meant giving up some freedom. The question before them: How committed were they? "I was worried about another company imposing its will on us," Dubinsky says. "But U.S. Robotics had cash, a great reputation with the retail channel, manufacturing strength, and global presence. And Touchdown was at a turning point. Was it going to be another nice gadget that failed? Or would it be the start of the next generation of computing?" Dubinsky and Hawkins made sure that Palm's 28 employees would be compensated, and fought long and hard over details about who would control manufacturing. At the end of the day, for $44 million in stock, Palm Computing became a division of U.S. Robotics.

The first order of business for the new company was to rename Touchdown. The Palm Pilot was born, and the first units shipped in April 1996. With U.S. Robotics distribution system, a wad of cash for promotion, and above all, a superior product, the rest was smooth sailing. "By midsummer, we couldn't build enough of them," Colligan remembers. "Customers were stamping their feet. And we weren't just selling to geeks in Silicon Valley. We were selling all over the place." The Palm Pilot became the fastest-selling consumer product in history—faster than the VCR, the color TV, the cell phone, even the personal computer. So successful was the Palm Pilot that in 1997, 3Com acquired U.S. Robotics in a deal valued at $7.8 billion. "This has been one of the great experiences of my life," says Ed Colligan. "You can't imagine how much fun it is to create a product that actually touches regular folks in their daily lives."

Each entrepreneur is unique, but the need for money is universal. Some entrepreneurs are like the gang at Procter & Gamble—businessminded men and women who innovate from inside a big corporation. Though a fairly rare species, the corporate entrepreneur is no less a risk-taker. When you put your budget and reputation on the line, failing can mean losing your job. Other entrepreneurs are like the folks at Palm—visionaries who chase often elusive venture capital money in search of a big payday. But the most common type of entrepreneur is the small-time innovator who has a great idea, yet whose lack of money is less important than their pluck and determination. Innovating this way is probably the most high-wire of capitalist acts. Failure usually means personal bankruptcy and a lot of very angry relatives. But when the idea works, it's like something straight out of a Horatio Alger rags-to-riches novel.

All in the Family
Funding the Production of Trivial Pursuit

Who lived at 221 B Baker Street? Sherlock Holmes, of course. Interest in obscure facts is nothing new. Television game shows are perhaps the best-known expression of people's unabated pursuit of trivia. One of the first of these having a broad appeal was the famous 1950s game show, *The $64,000 Question.* Question: What celebrity owes her fame to her appearance on that show? Answer: Dr. Joyce Brothers. Another popular quiz show at the time was *Twenty One,* whose best-known contestant was a professor from Columbia named Charles Van Doren. Television was forever changed when it was revealed that Van Doren was being fed the answers by the producers. For some, the ultimate trivia game show is *Jeopardy!,* hosted by Alex Trebec. With its quirky answer-before-the-question format, this long-lived quiz show amply demonstrates the public's continuing interest in trivia. Even the many incarnations of *Hollywood Squares* are evidence that ours is a culture that enjoys rattling off obscure facts and useless tidbits. And of course, we can't forget Regis Philbin and *Who Wants to Be a Millionaire.*

With this in mind, the interesting thing to note is that prior to Trivial Pursuit, there really were no board games that capitalized on this slightly under-the-radar craze, despite the fact that board games have been popular for eons. Take chess for example. The earliest clear ancestor of chess is the Indian game known as shaturanga. Invented by a sixth century Indian philosopher, it was a battle between four armies each under the control of a rajah, or king. Chinese chess is an offshoot of this game, the first reference of which has been found in a book called *The Book of Marvels* by Nui Seng-ju who died in 847 A.D. Backgammon-type games have been played for thousands of years in all parts of the world.

In the United States, probably the most famous board game of them all is Monopoly, invented by Charles Darrow. Once a salesman, he spent the early 1930s looking for a job. To fill his time, and help him forget his worries, Darrow invented things. One evening in 1930, Darrow sat down at his kitchen table and sketched out some of the street names of Atlantic City on the round piece of oilcloth that covered the table. He created houses and hotels for his little city, using scraps of wooden molding. He rounded up stray pieces of cardboard and typed out title cards for the different properties. The rest of the equipment was fairly easy to acquire, colored buttons for the tokens, a pair of dice, and a lot of play money.

From then on, to while away time in the evenings during the Great Depression, the Darrows would sit around the kitchen table buying, renting, developing, and selling real estate. They had little real cash on hand, yet "The Game," as they all referred to it, permitted them to manipulate large sums of money. As friends dropped in to visit, they were invited to join The Game, where it was quickly becoming a standard feature at the Darrow home. Encouraged by his friends, Darrow decided to test the game outside his sphere of acquaintants. He made up a few sets and offered them to department stores in Philadelphia, the nearest city. They sold.

In 1934, Darrow wrote to Parker Brothers, then, as now, one of the world's major game manufacturers and distributors. After testing the game for several weeks, Parker Brothers made the decision to reject it. Darrow then went to a printer friend, struck a deal, ordered the production of 5,000 sets, and started to sell the game locally. Orders came in and Darrow found himself working 14 hours a day just to keep up with the shipping. He wrote to Parker Brothers again, they reconsidered, and offered to buy the game outright and give Darrow royalties on all sets sold. The royalties from sales of Monopoly soon made Darrow a millionaire.

But by the late 1970s, board games were seen as a thing of the past. Monopoly was 50 years old, and Scrabble was even older. Successful new board games were just not being invented and marketed by the toy community. So, on December 15, 1979, when Chris Haney and Scott Abbot got together in Montreal to play a board game, they chose one of the very few available—Scrabble. Chris, nicknamed "Horn," is a high-school dropout who worked as a photo editor for the *Montreal Gazette.* His friend, Scott, is a bespectacled psychology graduate turned sportswriter for *The Canadian Press.* As they got out Chris's Scrabble game, they discovered that several of the pieces were missing. So they bought another Scrabble game, which got Chris thinking. He realized that this was the sixth game of Scrabble he'd bought throughout his life. The two friends decided then and there to invent a board game. As both were avid trivia buffs, a trivia game made the most sense. "It took us 45 minutes to design the game," says Scott, "and three months to figure out the scoring."

Getting a brainstorm is fantastic, but as the stories of the innovators in this book evidence, turning that idea into reality is much more difficult. This is even more true when the innovator knows nothing about the industry that he is embarking upon. Such was the fate of Chris Haney and Scott Abbot, two journalists who decided to enter the very competitive toy market. To say they were novices would be generous. While they had a "manic belief" in the game right from the start, they knew next to nothing about marketing and promotion. Fortunately, they were aware of their limitations (as opposed to the innovators who think they know it all). In January 1980, armed with an expired press pass and a camera without any film, the two buddies visited the Canadian Toy and Decoration Fair in Montreal posing as reporter and photographer. There, they pumped toy manufacturers to learn the strategies of marketing a game and, according to Scott, "collected about $10,000 worth of information in one afternoon."

The next step was to set up a company. The two knew early on that they would need some help, so they recruited Chris's older brother John, a one-time actor and former pro hockey player, and a lawyer friend, Ed Werner, to help them. Horn Abbot Limited was incorporated in January 1980, with Chris and Scott, the two founders, each receiving 22 percent of the company, and Ed and John each getting 18 percent. Because these were just ordinary guys with day jobs, families, and bills, there was not a whole lot of money available to get the product produced and distributed, so they decided to set 20 percent of the company aside for future barters.

With a trivia game in mind and a company formed, the next step was to write the actual questions. In October 1980, Chris packed a pile of almanacs, encyclopedias, guides, and record books, and left by boat for Spain with his wife Sarah and their two-year-old son. John joined them later, and for the next five months the brothers worked 16-hour days amassing mounds of trivia questions. They found questions wherever they looked. "Surprisingly, many questions are right in front of your nose," Chris points out. "How many Eskimos are there on the back of a Canadian two-dollar bill?" (Answer: Six.) The final editing of the questions, which took six weeks, was done in Ed Werner's dining room.

By this time, they felt that they were far enough along to commit to this risk full-time, so Chris quit his job and began contacting people who could manufacture different parts of the game. They hired an unemployed 18-year-old artist, Michael Wurstlin, to develop the board and logo, in exchange for five shares of the company. Everyone poured over color combinations and package designs. "They were meticulous in their attention to detail," says Joe Simpson, a manufacturing consultant who later printed the boxes and cards. "They knew exactly what they wanted and were going to get it, no matter how unorthodox." They rejected the usual flat game format, opting instead for a unique, chunky, square box. Then they spent weeks finding someone who would make a board to fit into the box. For the cover, they chose an elegant script that read "Trivial Pursuit." "We wanted it to look good on coffee tables, not just in toy cupboards," says Chris. By summertime, they began to get the game ready for a test run.

But to produce the first 1,200 copies, they needed money that they didn't have. What to do? Like most small entrepreneurs, they turned to friends and family. It's what Jeff Bezos did when he was trying to get Amazon.com off the ground, and it's what the four-person firm of Horn Abbot did when it wanted to get Trivial Pursuit off the ground. All four men went to the people they knew best, and eventually were able to badger 32 friends, relatives, and former colleagues into buying shares in the venture, raising about $60,000.

With some cash in hand, they were able to move the business out of their houses and into an office in downtown St. Catharines, Ontario. By the fall, the game components began to arrive, they all worked around the clock putting the boxes together, and by November they were ready to test their product. Says Scott, "We figured, if the game goes, fine. If it doesn't, we'll have Christmas presents for the rest of our lives." They shipped the first 1,100 boxes to stores in the Toronto area and a few to Vancouver. Each individual game cost Horn Abbot almost $75 to manufacture, an outlandish price for a board game, yet they decided to take a loss and sell each game initially for $15 so that retailers could price the game at $29.95—still a high price for a board game. All of the games quickly sold. Emboldened by their initial success, they took samples to the Canadian Toy and Decoration Fair but, to their dismay, sold only 200. They then went to the annual American International Toy Fair in New York, where things only got worse—144 orders. "At that point, we could have been had for a song," Chris acknowledges. He had exhausted his savings, had sold everything but his cameras, and had driven himself to anxiety attacks that forced a recuperation at his father-in-law's farm.

Yet, despite the ho-hum reaction by the toy community, people liked the game—a lot. If word of mouth is the best advertising you can get, then Trivial Pursuit was getting a lot of great advertising. Reorders from their initial retailers began to come in. But by this time, they had used up all of their capital and had no more games in stock. Sarah Haney, though six months pregnant, took a part-time nursing job to help pay the bills. The team went to banks for credit, but were turned down. "We'd really hit the bottom," recalls Chris. For several months they eked out a living on dwindling savings. Finally, they found a bank willing to give them a line of credit after Scott's father gave them a loan. Horn Abbot was in business for a little while longer, and this new infusion of cash allowed them to produce another 20,000 games. It was all or nothing now.

Needing a cheap place to assemble so many games, they turned an old boat-works into a make-shift factory. Scott decided to leave his job and become the company accountant, although he didn't even know what an invoice was. They used some of their precious cash to buy a computer because storing the questions on index cards didn't seem like such a hot idea. Games were shipped, the initial strong word of mouth held up, and orders began to pour into the small boat-works factory. The four-man team could barely keep up. With demand so high, despite the utter lack of an advertising or promotions budget and a distributor, it was clear that they were onto something.

They knew that if they could get an actual toy distributor interested, the game might really take off. Finally, in October 1981, they located Chieftain Products who, based on the amazing sales to date, agreed to handle distribution. Chieftain is a Canadian company and distributor for Selchow & Righter (ironically, the distributors of Scrabble), one of the largest games companies in the United States. Chieftain loved the game and sent it to the American company where three top executives played it, loved it too, and thought it might be their answer to the challenge of video games. In the meantime, prayers were answered when Chieftain ordered 80,000 games. Says Chieftain's Stew Robertson, "The snowball effect was incredible. The more we shipped, the greater the demand."

As Christmas approached, the snowball had turned into an avalanche. At Mr. Gameways' Ark in Toronto, the line of people waiting to buy the game stretched two aisles wide and outside the store. To handle the nonstop phone calls, Gameways had to set up a Trivial Pursuit hot line. The game soon became a national craze in Canada, with all of the attendant television and newspaper stories and sales. As the popularity of the game spread across Canada, Americans sought to cash in on the boom as well. In November, the creators signed a contract with Selchow & Righter to manufacture and distribute the game in the United States. The U.S. company hired a PR consultant who launched an unusual direct mail promotion to 1,800 of the top buyers attending the 1983 New York Toy Fair and to Hollywood stars. When Johnny Carson enthusiastically talked about the game on the Tonight Show, the game took off beyond anyone's wildest imagination. The camel's back had broke.

By the end of 1983, even before the Christmas rush, 2.3 million games of Trivial Pursuit had been sold in Canada, and a million more in the United States. Selchow & Righter could not keep up with the demand as retail sales soared that year. In 1984, a record 20 million games were sold in the United States alone, contracts were signed for European and Australian distribution rights, and retail sales exceeded $1 billion dollars. The kitchen table capitalists became media darlings. As Chris Haney said at the time, "Trivial Pursuit is taking over the world!" *Time* magazine put it another way, calling Trivial Pursuit "the biggest phenomenon in game history."

The paper chase is no less difficult for a big business than for a one-man show. Wooing angel investors or venture capital firms may be just as challenging as working a day job, tinkering in your shop at night, and selling your product on your own somewhere in-between. The difference may be that for the individual doing it all on his or her own, the risks of failure seem more personal and acute.

A Stroke of Genius
Liquid Paper's Artistic Beginnings

One thing all business innovators seem to have in common is that they have long marched to the beat of a different drummer. Each innovation that hits the big time probably represents the innovator's longstanding inbred need to do things his or her way. Bette Nesmith was no different. Raised in Dallas, Ms. Nesmith has been described by her sister, Yvonne, as a high-spirited girl who was "strong-willed and determined to do her own thing." At 17, Bette dropped out of high school. She married a year later, and a year after that, she became a mother at age 19 when her son Mike was born.

The fact that she couldn't type a whit didn't stop Ms. Nesmith from applying for a secretarial job with a prominent law firm. Impressed with her chutzpah, the firm hired her and sent her to secretarial school. Within a few years, her marriage ending, Ms. Nesmith went to work at the Texas Bank & Trust, in 1951. There she found a new breed of electric typewriter at her disposal. The manual typewriters she was familiar with used fabric ribbons, but these new machines used carbons ones. And, while a carbon ribbon made for a crisp and clean presentation, unlike with fabric ribbons, mistakes typed in carbon were almost impossible to erase. Even the most painstaking attempts to erase neatly left a telltale smudge. Smudges and bank letters did not go well together.

So Ms. Nesmith came upon a crafty solution to this common dilemma. Always the artistic sort, Nesmith realized while painting the bank's windows for the holidays, that she could easily paint over her mistakes, unlike the difficulty she had erasing typing errors. If she could do that on the bank's holiday window, why couldn't she do the same when typing? Bette Nesmith's million-dollar realization was that she could.

Ms. Nesmith took a small bottle of white tempera paint and a watercolor brush with her to work. The next time she mistyped a word, she simply painted over the mistake, waited for it to dry, fixed it, and typed on. No one was any the wiser. Her boss didn't notice, her peers didn't notice, no one noticed. For five years, she kept this her own private little secret. Says she, "Since I was correcting my mistakes with it, I was quiet about it."

But after a while, a great idea like this is bound to get around. Before long, secretaries in Nesmith's office were asking her for bottles of the correction fluid, and soon after that, every secretary in her building was using the stuff. When a local office supply dealer suggested that she market her idea, she realized that she might have a business in a bottle. She called her invention "Mistake Out" and began to sell it. Wanting a more catchy name, she soon changed the name to Liquid Paper and applied for a trademark. She also knew that she needed a patent, but being a single working mom, especially at a time when that was so rare, she couldn't afford a lawyer to help her apply for patent protection.

One thing Nesmith could do though was improve her product. The problem with tempera paint was that it was too thin and it dried too slowly. She knew that if she could make the product thicker and faster-drying, it wouldn't saturate the paper so much. Unable to afford a chemist, Nesmith decided to learn how to create the mixture herself. She went to the library and located a formula for tempera paint, and then went to Michael's school and spoke with his chemistry teacher to learn how to modify it. A trip to a paint factory taught her how to grind and mix the concoction correctly, and a few more field trips turned her into an amateur chemist.

At home in her kitchen, Ms. Nesmith began to experiment. Mixing different combinations of pigment, wetting agents, and resins eventually resulted in a formula with which she was satisfied. Her initial thought was to try to sell her product to a large company that had the resources necessary to manufacture and market the product properly. A friend knew someone in IBM's advertising agency in New York and offered to help. Nesmith put together a presentation package consisting of two typewritten letters. The first took 15 minutes to type, using an eraser to smudge-out mistakes. The second, an identical letter, took two and a half minutes to type cleanly, using Liquid Paper to fix the errors. IBM turned her down.

Then she had a dream. In her dream, Nesmith saw a clear image of a $700 invoice floating in the wind. To Bette Nesmith, the dream "was telling me to get busy." So busy she got. Despite being a single mother working a full-time job, she knew that the time had come for her to become a small businesswoman as well. Then she had an epiphany:

"As a young woman with a son to raise alone, I suffered greatly with extreme lack. I had tried to work this problem out by turning to God, but I never seemed to get anywhere until I was willing to humbly let go of my fear of, and dependency upon, matter."

With her spirit clear and a plan of action in place, Nesmith began her business in earnest. Her product was finally in a form that she was satisfied, if not thrilled, with, so she began to work on the packaging. Nesmith had packaged her fluid in a tube with an applicator tip, but this didn't seem quite right. She searched wholesalers and found a small plastic bottle that she liked; a bottle that would soon become a familiar sight in offices throughout the land. As 1958 approached, Nesmith's home-based business was selling 100 small bottles of Liquid Paper a month. And what a home-based business it was: Her kitchen was the chemistry lab and her garage was the storage and production facility. When orders would come in, she would hire her son Mike and his buddies to fill the little bottles with Liquid Paper. Though money was still tight, she scraped together $200 to hire a chemist to develop a faster-drying formula. He did, and Nesmith finally had the product that she had hoped for.

Like any enterprising small businesswoman, Bette Nesmith found customers where she could: in the phone book, through flyers, and by sending samples to local businesses and office supply stores. Word of mouth spread, and the business slowly grew. What Ms. Nesmith also knew was that if her business was to expand, a lot more people than she could ever afford to reach would need to hear about her product. Luckily for her, a free solution existed: the press.

The media, it has been said, is like a hungry elephant—it needs a ton of food every day, and that food is a new story. Newspaper editors and television producers have to come up with stories to fill their pages and airwaves, day after day, week after week, and it is not always easy to fill all that space.

Therefore, the entrepreneur that can make an editor's job easier by offering a great story about a new product is one that will get some free publicity. The benefits of getting your product mentioned in the press are twofold. First, it's free advertising. That alone is hard to beat. Second, a favorable review of a product is like an independent endorsement. Copy that article, duplicate that video, send it out, and credibility is yours.

And that is just what Bette Nesmith did. Sending samples of her product to various trade magazines resulted in some great publicity; publicity that no amount of money could have purchased. In October 1958, *The Office* prominently featured Liquid Paper in its "New Products of the Month" feature. More than 500 readers wrote in search of Nesmith's product. Soon thereafter, *The Secretary* published a similar item about Liquid Paper, creating even more demand.

But all of this business meant that Nesmith had to work late into the night, bottling the product, filling orders, sending out invoices, and generally running the business. Eventually, her night job began to affect her day job and she was fired from the bank. Though Nesmith's small Liquid Paper business was profitable, it wasn't enough to support herself and her son Michael, so she found a part-time job. This gave her time to travel around Texas to peddle her goods to office supply dealers. A trip to San Antonio was a turning point when a dealer ordered a gross, and then another, and then another.

Unlike some business tales, the Liquid Paper story to this point was not one where a dramatic breakthrough created a huge demand. Rather, it is like the story of most businesses—a good plan was well executed and the business showed steady growth. By 1962, after seven years in business, Nesmith was able to hire two part-time employees. Sales increased and Ms. Nesmith was able to secure a $500 loan that she used to buy a portable building to move the business into. Half of the 10-by-26-foot structure in Nesmith's backyard housed the office, and the other half was used for manufacturing and storage.

In 1963, Nesmith, along with her new husband, Bob Graham, decided that the time was right to hit the big leagues. The major trade show for the office supply industry was the National Office Products Association Convention, that year being held in Memphis, Tennessee. Trade shows are a great opportunity for business owners to promote, sell, network, and check out the competition—all in one location. Some presenters, understanding the importance of trade shows, budget large sums of money for their extravagant booths. The Grahams could not afford anything like that, instead opting to outfit the small Liquid Paper booth with a plant, a typewriter, a chair, and a painting borrowed from their local library. Yet whatever drawbacks their modest booth may have had, the product was exceptional and the reviews were great. Liquid Paper was on the map.

One thing that really helped spur the sales of Liquid Paper was that there was no competition. Bette Graham's product and business was small enough to fly under the competition's radar, yet large enough to grow at a steady clip. 1966 was a banner year for the once-single mother from Dallas. Not only were sales approaching the million-dollar mark, but her son Michael Nesmith had been tapped to star in a television show with three other lads, collectively known as The Monkees.

The growth of Graham's company from cottage industry to major corporation can be attributed to many factors, not the least of which was its unique product. But Graham credits other reasons. With a commitment to giving everyone who worked at the Liquid Paper Corporation a say in operations, Bette Nesmith Graham was at the forefront of a quiet revolution in the workplace. At a time when only the Japanese were known for group involvement in decision making, Graham's management stressed cooperative decision making. Everyone at the company, from secretaries through vice presidents, worked together on various joint committees, planning everything from new product development, to marketing, office operations, and manufacturing techniques. Says Graham, "Each employee's contribution was regarded as equal in importance and value."

By 1968, domestic grosses finally topped $1 million. In a speech to company employees, Graham said, "In 10 years we have come from production in a kitchen to a corporation employing many people. There have been many facets to our success—the ability to see a right idea, the stamina to work, the intelligence to plan, and the faith to measure progress by the good accomplished." That year, the company sold 1 million bottles of correction fluid. By 1970, that number had jumped to 5 million. In 1975, the company that began in Bette Nesmith's kitchen, moved into a 35,000-square-foot building in Dallas. The plant had equipment that could produce 500 bottles a minute, and in 1976, the Liquid Paper Corporation turned out 25 million bottles with net earnings of $1.5 billion. The company spent $1 million that year on advertising alone.

In 1976, Graham resigned as chairman of the board of Liquid Paper to devote herself to her religion and charities. In 1979, she sold her company to Gillette for $47.5 million dollars and royalties on every bottle sold through the year 2000.

The Innovation Rules

- Whether you are on your own or part of a large corporation, allocating the necessary resources is critical to the eventual success of the product.

- Resource allocation also requires funding new and improved versions of the product.

- Run a lean ship.

- Unless you are willing to strike out, you will not hit a home run.

5

!!!!!!!!!!!!!!!!!!!!!!!!!!

The Best Laid Plans of Mice and Men

Surprisingly, innovation can be a doubled-edged sword. For sure, the innovative product can bring riches and rewards, but just as easily, it might bring unwanted recognition and ruin. When you are so far ahead of the curve, you run the risk of running off the road. When that happens, presto! Your innovation is an albatross. Accordingly, another name for this chapter might as well be "What Not to Do."

The possibility for innovation miscalculation can take many forms. You may misjudge the market. What seems like an innovative product deserving of a big budget and a lot of secretive attention can turn out to be a boondoggle that no one wants. Is it really possible to be so wrong about the market? That a company as big as Coca-Cola did is a testament to that fact. Another miscalculation that occurs is when a true innovator opens the door for scores of imitators, but is not prepared to fend them off, is unable to distinguish his product from the others, or is unable to legally protect his idea. All his hard work and innovation is nothing more than free R&D for the jackals who will make a mint off his genius.

The business innovator is wise to heed the lessons in this chapter. Be diligent. Work hard. Be creative. Be bold.

But be a jerk too. Take a hard look at your innovation. Make sure that it is truly worthy of your time and best efforts. If you decide that it is, protect it. Hire the sharpest lawyer you can. Be ruthless. Don't let anyone steal your genius.

Pong
Giving Birth to a Video Nation

Throughout the 1960s, pinball games were all the rage. Yet a few short years later, the introduction of the first popular video game, Pong, made pinball all but obsolete. The impetus for the development of the video gaming industry, Pong almost single-handedly created both the home and the arcade video and computer game markets.

To understand the rise and fall of Pong, and Atari, the once-great company that developed it, we must begin at the beginning—with the very first computer game ever, "Spacewar." Programmed in 1962 by MIT student Steve Russell, Spacewar was a simple game, with graphics produced by an oscilloscope, where two players would blast lasers at each other's spaceships. The game ran on very large, very expensive, mainframe computers available only to a select few.

One of those who played this first-ever video game was a University of Utah undergraduate named Nolan Bushnell, playing Spacewar in the university's computer lab. So infatuated was he with the revolutionary game that Bushnell spent the next seven years trying to reproduce Spacewar, endeavoring to make it available as a coin-operated game. When it was finally completed in 1971, Bushnell's Spacewar variation, dubbed "Computer Space," was released by coin-op manufacturer Nutting Associates. It bombed. Not only was it too complicated, but it was so groundbreaking (remember, no one had ever seen a video game before) that people just were not interested in learning how to play it.

While Bushnell was busy trying to bring Spacewar to the arcade, an engineer named Ralph Baer was busy with a plan to bring a video game into the home. He began work in 1966 on what was to become the first-ever home video game system. One of the games Baer developed was a ball-and-paddle TV game. He licensed the game to Magnavox, and in 1972, Magnavox released Baer's brainchild as Odyssey—the first-ever home video game system. Magnavox started demonstrating the Odyssey system around the country at private showings. One of those shows was in Burlingame, a town near San Jose, California, and one of the people who attended the show was Nolan Bushnell. That little paddle and ball game really caught his eye.

Bushnell knew that his next game had to be much simpler than Computer Space, and he wanted to create a company to develop it. So he and partner Ted Dabny each put up $250 to create a parent company. Bushnell originally wanted to name the company Syzygy, but inexplicably, the name was already taken. Instead they named it Atari, a term used not coincidentally in the Japanese strategy game GO to politely warn an opponent that he is about to be conquered.

The first person Atari hired was a young engineer named Al Alcorn. Bushnell assigned him the job of developing a simple ball and paddle game. The prototype Alcorn created was simple indeed. On either side of the screen was a white bar, a paddle, about an inch long. A ball was launched from the center of the screen and the object of the game was to hit it back and forth. Bushnell remembers, "spending tremendous amounts of time trying to do things like calibrate how much a quarter turn of the control dial resulted in how much movement on the screen." They added a sound effect and reduced the instructions to six words: "Avoid missing ball for high score." The game was dubbed "Pong" for two reasons. First, it imitated the sound that the ball made when it hit the paddle, and second,

"Ping-Pong" had already been copyrighted. The first Pong arcade machine was placed in Andy Capp's bar in Sunnyvale, California, as a test.

The evening went like this:

One of the regulars approached the Pong game and studied the ball bouncing around the screen. A friend joined him. One of them inserted a quarter and there was a beep. They watched as a "ball" went from one side of the screen to the other. Each time it did the score changed. The game was tied at 3-3 when one player tried the knob controlling his paddle. The score was 5-4 when his paddle finally made contact with the ball. There was a "pong" sound and the ball bounced back to the other side of the screen. At 8-4, the second player figured out how to use his paddle. They had a brief volley just before the score went to 11-5. Game over.

Seven quarters later they were having extended volleys, and the pong noise was resonating through the bar and attracting the attention of others. Before closing, everybody had played the game. The next morning, a line had formed outside Andy Capp's before 10 A.M. to play Pong. But within a few days, the game had stopped working. Alcorn went down to the bar to figure out what went wrong, and discovered that the machine was crammed so full of quarters that it literally could not take any more.

Bushnell originally intended to sell Pong to Midway or Bally, but after that amazing test run, he decided that Atari should manufacture and distribute the game itself. It did, and to say that Pong went on to become a huge hit would be a vast understatement. College students became overnight addicts; in one week kids at the University of Miami pumped 3,000 quarters into one machine. The game was on television news shows, and bars couldn't get their hands on the new profit center fast enough. Within a year, Atari sold 8,500 machines. With arcade Pong such a massive success, Al Alcorn was eager to create a home version.

In 1974, Atari began work on Home Pong, a consumer version of the popular arcade game that could be played on a television set. Alcorn and engineer Bob Brown developed the product. Yet once it was completed, Atari needed a distribution partner because it could not afford to market the product alone. Atari was not a company with $50 million in venture capital or $100 million in IPO money. It was a small shop started by two guys and $500 bucks. As such, money was a constant concern. Says Bushnell, "Atari was an all-consuming entity. And part of it was this chase for capital, this quest for payroll. Because it was perpetually undercapitalized. I was always trying to make payroll. You can tell the difference between an employee and an entrepreneur by the way they look at payroll. If they look forward to it, they're an employee. If they hate it, they're an employer."

But because of Odyssey's poor sales, no retailers were interested in carrying the Atari Home Pong console. Finally, in 1975, after being turned down by toy, electronics, and department stores, an Atari executive reached Tom Quinn at Sears. After several meetings with Bushnell, Sears ordered 150,000 Home Pong consoles for Christmas. Home Pong was released in 1975 and quickly became the best-selling item in the Sears catalog (which was a big deal at the time). The national exposure Sears gave Atari helped catapult Bushnell's company to international success. Atari, through its Atari 2600 home video console, became the fastest-growing business in U.S. history.

But despite initial success, problems occurred almost immediately. Other companies began flooding the market with Pong-like games. In no time, 20 different ping-pong games were on the market. And Magnavox began suing left and right, because it owned the copyright to Odyssey—the game that inspired Pong. Atari ended up paying Magnavox over $700,000. Even worse, Atari set itself up for more problems by not trademarking the Pong name until Pong clones were already on the market. Thus, several companies cloned Pong, used the name, and sold it at a lower price. Others tried to improve on it by adding separate controls, support for four-player games, color, and changes in speed. Pong's phenomenal success created a runaway bandwagon.

Although Pong was soon viewed as too simple, in the late 1970s Pong and Atari were still number one. But with several new games in the works for Atari, Bushnell decided to get out while the getting was good. He was offered $28 million from Warner for the company and took it. He stayed on as chairman of the board, but left Atari two years later a rich man.

Bushnell had gotten out at the right time because the getting wasn't good for very much longer. By the late 1970s, a new generation of much more sophisticated computer games was in the works at the many Atari imitators. Pong would soon become a relic of a bygone era. At the same time, Warner was having a hard time getting Atari's other products out the door and began to lose money on the venture. Explains Bushnell, "What happened at Atari is that Warner continued to coast up to $2 billion in sales but nobody there that was left really understood why. They kind of thought it was their brilliance. But what really happened is the products had been created, and it was just a matter of marketing them. When it came time to introduce a new product, they essentially wouldn't let anything out of the lab that didn't match an unrealistic hurdle rate. And so, as a result, if you're not introducing new stuff, you die. It was really sad to see." By 1983, Atari lost $538 million. Warner eventually sold the company, and the Atari brand name, once a corporate identity second only to Coca-Cola, became a footnote in the gaming industry.

It was a short, wild ride. Atari, the late great game maker, couldn't compete in the percolating personal computer market. The demise of Atari proved that it is possible to be too successful. What could it have done differently? Obviously, its failure to protect its name and its intellectual property was a horrendous blunder. The Atari brand in general, and the Pong name in particular, were valuable assets. To allow Pong to be bastardized by its competition was a gaffe of the first order. That failure alone allowed imitators to cash in on its innovation and undermine the company. An attorney who didn't trademark the Pong name is an attorney who committed malpractice. So the lesson is this: When you innovate, you need not litigate. Protect your intellectual property by filing for the appropriate copyright, trademark, or patent and you are well on your way.

By the same token, Atari was a company that was also severely undercapitalized. Cash is the lifeblood of any company. Having money in the bank enables you to expand, advertise, outfox your competitors, or otherwise handle business, whatever your priorities. When cash was needed, the pre-Warner Atari was unable to operate properly. Faced with a slew of cheap Pong imitators, Atari should have been able to crush them. Instead, it was forced to sell out to Warner.

Finally, the Warner version of Atari became overconfident, resting on its laurels at a time when competition was fierce. When you innovate, you run the very real risk that a flood of competitors will come out from under the rocks to leech off of your success. You have to stay one step ahead of the competition. For example, Microsoft is a company that takes nothing for granted. It innovates, and then sets about topping itself. That is why you see new versions of Windows every few years. Just imagine what Pong could have evolved into had Atari continued to expand. Instead it retracted. Had things been handled differently, Atari could have become Nintendo instead of Edsel.

Innovation is allegedly a prized commodity in the business world. Companies are supposed to encourage it, but many do not, and it is not hard to see why. Some businesses are of the belief that it is better to bet on the devil you know than the devil you don't. Innovation means change, and change is not always welcome. Who knows what will be wrought by the change? Sometimes it is great, and sometimes it's a disaster.

Cola War Casualty
The Backlash Against New Coke

Coca-Cola first appeared in Atlanta, Georgia, when Dr. John Pemberton used a three-legged brass pot to concoct a medicinal elixir in 1886. In the ensuing 100 years, Coke would go from a small regional drink to a worldwide behemoth. It became easily one of the most recognizable, if not *the most* recognizable brand in the world. It can be found almost anywhere on the planet—from the Serengeti Plain of Africa to the smallest village in Asia to any street corner in the United States. And by 1985, on the eve of its centennial anniversary, Coke and its chairman Roberto Goizueta had witnessed a remarkable set of new accomplishments: The acquisition of Columbia Pictures in January 1982 and the introduction of Diet Coke later that August were foremost among them. Thus, on the face of things, the company's decision in 1985 to change the formulation of its flagship product, its bread and butter, the king of the hill, the heavyweight product champion of the world—Coca-Cola—seems inexplicable, inconceivable.

But when you dig deeper, you see that Coca-Cola faced tremendous problems in the 1980s, despite its worldwide reputation. The baby boom generation is a group that has tried to hold on to its collective youth. In the early 1980s,

Coke's biggest competitor, Pepsi, tapped into this sentiment with an advertising campaign touting Pepsi as "the
choice of a new generation." And it worked; Coke's hold on
the top spot began to slip. The battle between Coca-Cola
and Pepsi-Cola was dubbed the "Cola Wars," and Coke was
losing.

Another front of this war was the so-called "Pepsi Challenge"—a head-to-head taste test whereby cola drinkers
were asked to compare the tastes of two colas, not knowing
which was which. Needless to say, the television ads always
showed Pepsi winning the taste test. Effective advertising,
but even more troubling was that the tests were real. People
did enjoy the taste of Pepsi more in blind taste tests. On top
of that, in November 1983, Pepsi paid Michael Jackson the
then unheard of sum of $5 million to make two commer-
cials for Pepsi. Pepsi really seemed to be the choice of a new
generation.

The data confirmed this: Coke was losing market share.
Coke's lead had dropped from a better than two-to-one mar-
gin to a mere 4.9 percent lead by 1984. In supermarkets,
Coke was trailing by 1.7 percent. Moreover, Coke's overall
market share fell from 24.3 percent in 1980 to 21.8 in 1984.
As Pepsi USA President Roger Enrico boasts, "For 20 years,
we used this Pepsi Generation campaign to reach out not
just to the young but to all people who look forward, who
are curious about the next thing, who wanted more out of
life." As a result, by the mid 1980s, Coke was looking a bit
stodgy; it seemed to represent nostalgia and small towns,
parades, and picnics. The problem was that this image
would not necessarily appeal to the younger constituency of
soft drinkers who dominate the market. Coke was clearly in
danger of becoming the number two soft drink.

That would be remarkable. Like the stars and the moon,
Coca-Cola was a fact of life. Possibly the greatest brand in
history, Coke was, and is, an institution. Its formula, "Mer-

chandise 7X" is so secret that at one time the company decided to pull out of India (with its one billion thirsty inhabitants) rather than disclose the formula to the Indian government. As Pepsi chairman Enrico put it, "Merchandise 7X was not just a mixture of sugar and flavoring—it was an alchemical concoction. And the soft drink it produced was not just a thirst-quencher. It was the one unchanging taste in a world that changed more rapidly than anyone would have wished."

Yet Coke was slowly losing ground to Pepsi, despite the fact that Coke was far outspending Pepsi on advertising—by upwards of $100 million per year. One major problem was that the Pepsi Challenge had been fabulously successful: Pepsi's share jumped 8 points since the inception of the campaign. So Coke's continued market domination seemed largely due only to its greater availability. The difference in share, according to Coke's own market research department, was that if someone wanted Pepsi, she might only find Coke. Essentially, McDonald's was propping up Coke. Roy Stout, at the time the head of market research for Coca-Cola USA, put it this way: "If we have twice as many vending machines, dominate fountains, have more shelf space, spend more on advertising, and are competitively priced, why are we losing share? You look at the Pepsi Challenge, and you have to begin asking about taste."

It was a radical idea, changing the taste of Coca-Cola. You might as well ban baseball and outlaw apple pie while you're at it. Yet sometimes even the craziest ideas seem to make sense. It may be because you are in a vacuum and only hear the voices of those close to you, or that you see no alternative. For Coke, its decision to play with its centennial-old secret formula seemed to be a combination of converging factors. Brian Dyson, president of Coca-Cola USA, said at the time, "maybe the principal characteristics that made Coke distinctive, like its bite, consumers now describe as harsh . . . [m]aybe the way we assuage our thirst has changed." By the fall of 1983, Coke's top brass allowed Dyson and Stout "to explore the possibility of a reformulation." Dyson chose Sergio Zyman, senior vice president of marketing of Coca-Cola USA, to head the project.

Zyman was discouraged by much of the market research conducted between 1983 and 1985 on the possibility of a new Coke. One set of focus groups said that while it would be fine for Pepsi to improve its formula, Coke could not. It was, after all, Coke. "It was like saying you were going to make the flag prettier," says Zyman. Other problems emerged. When asked, "What is your favorite drink?" most people said, "Coke." Yet when asked, "What do you drink?" the response was sometimes Coke, sometimes Pepsi, sometimes whatever was on sale.

But in September 1984, the geniuses at Coke thought they had found the answer. The technical division had brewed a formula of Coke that beat Pepsi in blind taste-tests, by up to 8 points. Previously, Pepsi had beaten Coke by anywhere from 8 to 15 points. The new formulation meant, at a minimum, an 16-point swing. According to Dyson, "The minute we had the product, Coca-Cola USA said let's set it in motion."

There is no gentle way to put this: That was one of the stupidest business decisions in the annals of stupid business decisions. Coca-Cola has been the most successful product in history, the undisputed leader of the $25 billion soft-drink industry. While a number of adjustments had been made in Coke's proportions of sugar and caffeine since 1886, Merchandise 7X had never been changed. Unlike almost every other product, the one thing Coke never was, was new. But Coke executives were allayed by the fact that overhauling the ingredients of a popular product happens all the time. Whenever you see "new and improved" on a label it means that something has changed. The difference with Coke was that it is one of the most successful products in the history of the world. How can you improve upon that?

Frito-Lay certainly understood this. Years ago, sales of Fritos took a sudden dive, for no apparent reason. Frito-Lay hired a slew of experts and consultants to do their requisite analyses and reports. Advertising was changed, heads rolled, nothing changed. Finally, it was discovered that some middle management executives had slightly changed the Fritos recipe. When top management found out, the original recipe was immediately restored. Crisis solved. This story and its moral became part of the training for all new incoming Frito-Lay management. The moral they were told was this: "Don't f**k with Fritos." It was a lesson that Coke would have to learn the hard way.

Now Coca-Cola did not go into this decision willy-nilly. Its research on the new product was one of the most exhaustive market research projects in history. Costing more than $4 million, Coke interviewed almost 200,000 consumers. Coke says that in blind taste tests, results indicated that 55 percent of those surveyed preferred New Coke. When told they were drinking two varieties of Coca-Cola, the preference shot up to 61 percent. Management made sure that the taste test results were checked, double-checked, and then corroborated in every major market in the country.

On April 23, 1985, New Coke was released with a great deal of fanfare. Announcing the new formula, Coca-Cola President Goizueta called his decision, "the surest move ever made." A more apt description of the decision comes from former Pepsi chairman Roger Enrico who says, "the other guy blinked."

The reaction to New Coke was swift and strong. People hated the stuff, hated the thought that they could never drink "old" Coke again, and hated the company for taking it away from them. The Coca-Cola Company suddenly became something of a national joke. Late-night television hosts derided the new product. People had pangs of desire for the old stalwart. In Beverly Hills, a wine merchant bought 500 cases of old Coke and started selling them for $50 a case. He sold out in a few days. Cokeaholics began stockpiling old Coke in their homes. One Hollywood producer rented a $1,200 wine cellar to hold his 100 cases of old Coke. Seattleite Gary Mullins started the Old Coke Drinkers of America and 8,500 people joined. One columnist called Coke executives "soda jerks," and more than one pleaded with Coke management to bring back old Coke. By mid-June 1985, the Coke consumer hotline was taking 1,500 irate calls a day. That same month, local Coca-Cola bottlers signed a petition demanding the return of old Coke.

A hungry populace was yearning to be free from New Coke. A groundswell, nay a tsunami, of popular sentiment arose demanding that old Coke be reintroduced. And a company heard their cries. Unfortunately for Coca-Cola, that company was Pepsi. Says Enrico, "What would *you* do if you were running the second-largest company in your industry, and the largest trashed its biggest-selling product? First, you'd be amazed. We were. Then you'd have some fun at their expense." So Pepsi researchers were told to crack the code that was Merchandise 7X. And they did, in about three days. If Coca-Cola wouldn't give the public what it wanted, Pepsi would. It was set to introduce "Savannah Classic Coke" in September 1985.

But Coke had already learned its hard lesson. A mere two months after its disastrous innovation, the company was already planning to reintroduce old Coke. On July 10, 1985, Coke executives made a remarkable announcement: "We want people to know we are sorry for any discontent we have caused them for almost three months. We have hurt you, and for that we are sorry." They then announced that old Coke, or Coca-Cola Classic as it would now be called, was back. "Coca-Cola Classic is truly a celebration of loyalty," they said. When Coca-Cola announced that it would bring back old Coke, Democratic Senator David Pryor of Arkansas called Coke's capitulation "a very meaningful moment in the history of America. It shows that some national institutions cannot be changed."

So just what went wrong? Begin with the research. First of all, amazingly, the Coca-Cola Company did no test marketing; it never actually tried out the new formula in a few cities to see how people would react to it. Even worse, they never explained to people, in all Coke's $4 million worth of research, that liking New Coke meant that there would be no old Coke. Yet it is true that considerable attention was devoted to testing consumer reactions to the idea of changing Coke's flavor. Coca-Cola consumers were asked a long series of questions about what their reactions to such a change would be: Would you be upset? Would you try the new drink? Would you switch brands immediately? Coca-Cola estimated from the response that 10 percent to 12 percent of exclusive Coke drinkers would be upset, and that half of those would get over it, and half wouldn't. But they figured that the alienation would fade away. What they did not count on was that this alienated core would stir discontent that would lead them to have to reintroduce old Coke. In the end, while the interviews pointed to people's willingness to try a new Coke, no one ever thought that Coca-Cola would actually tamper with its core product, its very identity, in the process.

Were there less drastic alternatives to the challenges faced by Coke in the early 1980s Cola Wars? Pepsiman Enrico says that Coke should have simply changed its advertising strategy, not its basic formulation. He points to Wheaties as an example of another standard-bearer that remains new and vibrant because its advertising is new and vibrant. Coca-Cola could have simply changed its ad campaigns to give Coke a younger image because image is probably more important than taste in selling soda pop.

Yet Coca-Cola made the most drastic of moves, innovating when innovation was the very worst thing it could have done. Why? Because they were desperate to change. When Goizueta became chairman in 1981, he was determined to be the chairman of change. He promised there would be "no sacred cow in the way we manage our business, including the formulation of any or all of our products." His aggressive attitude helped reinvigorate what had become a sluggish company. Goizueta was the first to put the sacred Coke name on a new product for the first time when he introduced Diet Coke in 1982. In early 1985, he put the Coke name on another new product, Cherry Coke. Goizueta had choreographed the purchase of Columbia Pictures in 1982. He and other executives were getting caught up in the success of their previous changes and decided to make one grand decisive move to recapture the soft-drink market they were losing to Pepsi.

Another option would have been to simply introduce New Coke without knocking out old Coke. There were a number of very good reasons why this never happened. First, the bottlers let it be known that they were not interested in adding another product to an already bloated line. Coke had just added Diet Coke, Caffeine-Free Diet Coke, Caffeine-Free Coke and Cherry Coke. The top brass was also pushing for the addition of Diet Cherry Coke and Minute Maid Orange Soda. These new products increased bottler costs tremendously.

Coca-Cola management was also worried about the interaction between two brands. They were worried that a new Coke would cannibalize the sales of old Coke, or vice versa. A new Coke would also invite comparisons between the two Cokes in the media and the public, and that would ultimately hurt the sales of both brands. Which brand would

McDonald's choose? Why didn't it choose the other one? Ultimately, Goizueta decided that the costs of two Cokes far outweighed the benefits. Old Coke would have to go.

But what Coca-Cola executives failed to realize is that there's more to marketing soft drinks than winning taste tests. Consumers have an emotional attachment to some products. "We did not understand the deep emotions of so many of our customers for Coca-Cola," said President Donald R. Keough. "It is not only a function of culture or upbringing or inherited brand loyalty. It is a wonderful American mystery. A lovely American enigma. And you cannot measure it any more than you can measure love, pride, or patriotism."

It is an interesting footnote that no one at Coca-Cola was fired after this debacle. The same top management team of Goizueta, Keough, and Dyson continued for a number of years until Dyson moved on to head Coca-Cola's company-owned bottling operations. Why was this? First of all, remarkably, Coke did not lose money as a result of this fiasco. In fact, the stock price jumped from $61.875 to $84.500, a 35.5 percent increase. By early 1986, the stock had reached an all-time high of $110. Goizueta was rewarded with $1.7 million in salary and bonuses for 1985, and was additionally awarded an almost $5 million bonus for the increase in stock price. President Keough's wage was more than $3 million.

According to Coca-Cola's 1986 proxy statement, these awards were given for "singular courage, wisdom, and commitment in making certain decisions in 1985 which entailed considerable business risks, the net result of which has been, and will continue to be, extremely beneficial to the shareholders of the company." Herbert A. Allen, chairman of Coke's compensation committee, said, "They had the courage to put their jobs on the line, and that's rarely done today at major American companies." Roger Enrico argues that a mass firing would have essentially put everyone at Coca-Cola on notice that risk-taking would be punished.

Maybe the most amazing thing that resulted from all this, the reason why management was promoted instead of sacked, was that, remarkably, this debacle ended up greatly *helping* Coca-Cola. For one surprisingly glorious, albeit quite painful summer, Coke made headlines all across the country. People organized to save their favorite drink. They even tried to file a class action suit to keep it around. Best of all, many people were reminded that their favorite things don't always last forever. Coke became a prized commodity. Ultimately, and partly as a result of the bad taste New Coke left in people's mouths, Coca-Cola won the Cola Wars. In spite of itself, today Coke still has more shelf space, more fountain outlets, and more advertising than Pepsi.

One thing that can be said in Coke's favor is that it swung for the fences. The fact is that when you try to hit a home run odds are greatest that you will strike out. This is as true in business as it is in baseball. Coca-Cola, when faced with a dangerous erosion in sales and reputation, spared no expense once it decided on its bold new path (however odd the decision seems in retrospect), and it still whiffed. Even with all of that money behind it, New Coke failed to be the real thing.

Imagine the problems then faced by the company that doesn't have the money Coca-Cola has. Coke can strike out and still play ball, but not everyone else can. Many necessary things must come together for an innovative product to become a commercial hit. You must have the right idea at the right time, you must execute it correctly, and you must have the money required to do it right. Capital is the lifeblood of any business. Without it, bad things—very bad things—can happen.

Mismanaging Innovation
The Collapse of DeLorean

When you look at a DeLorean, what stands out most are the doors—those beautiful gull-wing doors. Fully opened, the doors give the car the look of an X-wing fighter from *Star Wars*. Unlike the gull-wing doors of the 1956 Mercedes-Benz 300SL or a Bricklin, the DeLorean DMC-12 doors require only 14 inches of swing space, which comes in handy in a tight parking spot or when opening the door into traffic. Such economy, compared with the 40 inches or more required by most conventional car doors, makes the doors not only distinctive, but practical.

Technically, the DeLorean is a solid, if underperforming automobile, powered by a Peugeot-Renault-Volvo V-6 engine and a Bosch fuel-injection system. It sits on a Lotus-designed chassis and features independent four-wheel suspension. It has a wide, 62-inch wheelbase, with its front wheels an inch smaller in diameter than its back ones for better handling. It purrs. There is no doubt that this car was engineered for the driving enthusiast.

But what draws most people to the DeLorean has little to do with its powertrain or suspension. The attraction isn't what's under the hood. It's the design. Giorgetto Giugiaro of Ital Design studios in Turin, Italy, was recruited to create a unique look for the DeLorean. Giugiaro had designed such notable autos as the Maserati Bora, the Alfa Romeo Giulia Sprint GT, Volkswagen's Scirocco, and the Lotus Esprit, and that is why John DeLorean hired Giugiaro to design his signature automobile. Even today, some 20 years after the DeLorean made its splashy debut and dramatic fall, the brushed-steel car is still a thing of beauty.

It's been 20 years since John Z. DeLorean challenged the automotive industry with his so-called ethical sports car shipped from a state-of-the-art factory in Dunmurry, Northern Ireland. The history of DeLorean Motor Company is a daring, turbulent, and disastrous one, which left a lasting stigma on its founder, a slew of disgruntled investors, and a battery of lawyers in its wake. It is a hard lesson in economics for any would-be innovator.

John DeLorean was meant to be a car man. Born in 1925 on Detroit's east side, he was the son of a Ford employee and his first-ever job was with Chrysler. He left there and went on to Packard Motor Co. and then on to General Motors as Pontiac's Director of Advanced Engineering. DeLorean happened upon Pontiac at a fortuitous time; the company was in the midst of throwing off its image as a maker of cars for old ladies and was trying to reinvent its brand as something new and hip. In one of his first acts, DeLorean dumped a huge engine into a Pontiac Tempest, renamed it, and thereby helped create the soon-to-be-legendary Pontiac GTO. When the GTO debuted in 1964, Pontiac sold an astounding 31,000 cars, and 312,000 more over the next four years. The remarkable sales record of the GTO single-handedly saved the Pontiac division, changed the carmaker's image, and branded DeLorean a wunderkind, albeit a maverick wunderkind.

At age 40, he was made a GM vice president and general manager of Pontiac. Four years later, his meteoric star continued to rise when he was named the youngest ever general manager of Chevrolet. Under DeLorean's reign, Chevrolet's profits zoomed, up 400 percent in four years. He was promoted to the position of vice president of GM's American car and truck divisions in 1973, where he was expected to become GM's next president. But it was quickly apparent that DeLorean was just too wild for the button-down GM crowd. His double-breasted suits, long hair, and numerous wives didn't fit the corporate bill, and as a result, he and GM parted ways in 1973.

With his corporate life now behind him, DeLorean set out to achieve his ultimate dream, to develop his own car and company. According to DeLorean, "The goal was to design and build a car that would be as safe as possible, reliable, comfortable, handle and perform well, be enormous[ly] fun to drive and unmistakably elegant in appearance." In 1975, the DeLorean Motor Company (DMC) was founded, and financed, at least in part, by the likes of Johnny Carson, Sammy Davis, Jr., and, most improbably, the British government. Great Britain financed the factory DeLorean needed after he played one country off another, shopping his car around like Al Davis while looking for a new city for the Raiders. In fact, DMC was on the verge of signing a deal with Puerto Rico when the British-backed Northern Ireland Development Agency came up with a finance package that beat all others.

Just consider that for a moment. Say you are a wealthy unconventional automaker hell-bent on making a sports car for the masses, and you can pretty much choose any place on the planet to build it. Of all places, why in 1975 would you choose Belfast, Northern Ireland? Of course, the answer is dollars, 140 million of them to be exact. In an effort to improve employment in war-torn Belfast, the British government figured that having a major automobile factory would help the economy, and sure enough it did. DeLorean Motor Cars, Ltd. (DMCL), the division of DMC that assembled the cars and supplied DMC with most of its money, would eventually employ 2,600 workers.

Yet, while the state-of-the-art Irish car factory was being built on time, the development of the car became a tortured tale of misspent money, ineptitude, greed, and theft. Developing a workable prototype took far longer and cost more—much more—than DeLorean and his backers ever anticipated. Prototypes were created and abandoned. Millions were spent and wasted. Backers were getting nervous, and still no car. After talking to Porsche and BMW, DeLorean finally settled on troubled automaker Lotus to design the chassis and outside paneling. But Lotus decided to scrap much of the work that had been done in the preceding four years and start from scratch. This in turn infuriated DeLorean, who refused to let Lotus finish the project, deciding instead that the carmaker was far too slow to create the car he wanted. Production was stalled again. Money was tight and DeLorean was in a hurry. Finally, out of sheer desperation, fast Johnny hired a group of retired hotshot American engineers to take the project over. They were able to take the car from prototype to production in six months, but the money was quickly evaporating.

As this circus played itself out, DeLorean was not content to sit and wait. At various times during the production fiasco, he was linked to plans to buy Jeep, acquire Lotus, purchase American Motors, buy Alfa Romeo, buy Lancia, purchase Chrysler, merge with Ford, do a deal with Mitsubishi, explore for oil, import diesel engines, build cars in Poland, acquire the rights to the Sterling Engine, buy a bank, and even sell CB radios. DeLorean was fiddling as Rome burned.

Initially planned to debut in 1978, the DeLorean Sports Car was finally unveiled three years and many millions of dollars later, in 1981. Certainly it was an eye catcher: With those gull-wing doors and that rust-proof stainless steel body outside, and leather seats, power windows and mirrors, and an adjustable steering wheel inside, the car was unlike anything on the road at the time. But it was also overpriced ($26,600, when it had been projected to come in at $12,000), too heavy, and underpowered, all of which caused critics to give it less than rave reviews.

Buyers' opinions of the car widely varied. Many complained that the performance was not as powerful as they had been led to believe, and worse, many found that their cars had serious problems. Dick Brown, who ran the two quality assurance centers for DMC, was forced to totally rebuild many of the first cars. Yet even with these problems, the DeLorean was an international hit, sort of like the movie that gets so much advance attention, people see it despite the reviews. In its first year, DMCL actually increased production to 400 cars per week, but problematically, this was far more than the 1981 sports car market could bear. Even so, DMCL was the only British car company to make a profit in 1981.

But for every 1981 there is a 1982. With the DeLorean no longer the flavor of the month, press reports turned sour, dissatisfied customers made news, and sales dropped precipitously. Unfortunately, because DMC had burned through its capital at such a furious rate, it had nothing in its reserve cash tank. Desperate to keep things afloat, DMC executives struggled to find financial support, with DeLorean leading the way. All efforts were rebuffed and the British government was forced to put DMCL into receivership in July of that year. Receivership is a process in which a receiver is appointed to come in and run a failing company in an effort to fix its problems, and, undoubtedly, DMC had its share of problems. Sir Kenneth Cork was appointed to be the DMC receiver, having successfully saved several other major companies. The British government was counting on him to save their huge investment in DMCL.

In the meantime, John DeLorean was scrambling to keep the dream alive, and that meant finding money, lots and lots of money. With the British government threatening foreclosure, DeLorean became more desperate. It is against this backdrop that his former neighbor, James Hoffman, proposed a scheme that he said would net DeLorean $15 million. DeLorean was all ears. And that is how John DeLorean came to be in a seedy Los Angeles motel room in October 1982, caught on videotape calling the mass of cocaine in front of him "as good as gold," and why he was arrested and charged with trafficking cocaine.

What DeLorean didn't know was that Hoffman was a convicted felon turned government informant who was working for the feds in a sting operation. At trial in 1984, DeLorean's counsel argued that the automaker had been set up by the government and was a victim of entrapment. The jury agreed, and acquitted DeLorean of all charges. But that was not the end of his, or his company's, legal problems. DMC soon filed bankruptcy, DeLorean was indicted on fraud and racketeering charges in Detroit, he faced criminal charges in Great Britain, and his wife left him. It would take another ten years for the legal mess to sort itself out. It is estimated that DeLorean spent upwards of $8 million on legal fees defending himself against everyone from the United States government to ex-lawyers to his brother Charles, a DeLorean-Cadillac dealer in Cleveland.

When the DeLorean Motor Company collapsed, various people were left holding the bag that had once held John DeLorean's innovative dream. Workers in Northern Ireland, 365 dealers who had signed up to sell the car, the British government, celebrity investors—every last one, out of luck.

It would be a potshot to say that the lesson here is that innovation requires sufficient capital; that's obvious. Of maybe more import is the lesson below the surface, sort of like the car beneath the shell. While the DeLorean looked great, it wasn't. It was an average car that was slow and underperformed—not exactly what you want from a luxury sports car. And therein lies the real lesson. If you are going to take the time and expend the effort to create something new, do it right. Create a product that is great, that does what it is supposed to do, that does what you promise it will do. If you do that, there will never be a need to conduct business from a motel room near LAX.

Few things have been more innovative in the recent past than computers. Always quicker, smaller, and cheaper, computers have become innovation incarnate. Because whole books could be (and have been) written on this subject, they have purposefully been left out of this book. But when it comes to grand failures, one story needs to be remembered.

Lisa
Computing's Most Innovative Failure

Apple Computer was founded in Los Altos, California, in 1976, and by 1978 it was the world's fastest growing computer company. With the Apple II, the company had revolutionized the nascent home-computer market. For an encore, the company was working on a new computer, code-named Lisa. Officially, Apple states that *Lisa* stood for local integrated software architecture. Unofficially, Lisa was said to be named after the daughter of Steve Jobs, Apple's cofounder. Whatever the case, plans for the computer changed radically when, late in 1979, Jobs visited the Xerox Corporation's Palo Alto Research Center (PARC). So moved was he by what he saw that day, that he went back a second time; visits that changed the world.

In many ways, modern computing began at PARC, and what really caught Jobs's eye was a prototype machine called the Alto. The Alto had features never before seen on any computer. What made it truly unique was its graphical user interface. At a time when most computer users, including users of the Apple II, communicated with their machines via a series of arcane instructions typed into a keyboard, the Alto used a mouse (see Chapter 6), which allowed users to point and click on little pictures, or "icons." No computer was ever so easy to use.

PARC was a remarkable place. It was responsible for the development of the laser printer; on-screen graphics; "what you see is what you get" editing of memos, e-mail, illustrations, and animations; the menu commands Cut, Copy, and Paste; and overlapping windows with scroll bars. Some of the PARC work was first commercialized in the Xerox Star, a 1981 system that featured a two-button mouse. Jobs was convinced that he had seen the future of personal computing, and its name was the Alto. But the suits from Xerox thought that all of these bells and whistles made the computer cost-prohibitive. At an estimated $40,000 per unit, the Alto was never meant to be mass-produced. Xerox thought it was an unmarketable, albeit enthralling, anomaly.

But Jobs was a true believer and he and his team at Apple set about to incorporate the spirit of Alto's user interface into the Lisa. The plan was to build a revolutionary computer that would be easy to use, pleasing to look at, intuitive, and reliable. It would conform to the ways people actually worked, have enough power to do the tasks that need to be done, and fit into an everyday work environment. This was a tall order, especially in the prehistoric computer days of 1979. Steve Jobs is nothing if not ambitious.

The Lisa was to have a large (for the time) 12-inch black-and-white screen, two floppy disk drives (called Twiggy), lots of memory, and most amazingly, a mouse and icons. The development of the Lisa was a tremendous undertaking for Apple and essentially required most of the company's financial and personnel resources. Apple reports that Lisa cost $50 million to develop and required 200 man-years of development effort. Lisa made its debut on January 19, 1983.

A unique marvel it was. Consumers, used to seeing white (or sometimes blue) typeface upon a black screen, often reading "file unknown," were amazed to see on Lisa a little manila folder and wastebasket. Bundled with Lisa was a suite of sophisticated software, including a word processor, spreadsheet, and a paint program. For the first time, a commercially available computer featured pull-down menus, keyboard shortcuts, menu commands named New, Open, Close, Save, and Print, windows that zoomed open and closed, pictures that moved by pointing and clicking, boxes to provide warnings and explain errors, and a printer, the Image Writer. But all of this came at a price—each Lisa sold for $9,995.

Needless to say, Apple had high hopes for Lisa, but there were problems with the machine from the very start, not the least of which was the $10,000 price tag. Because of its technological sophistication and memory needs, the Lisa was heavy (48 pounds) and slow. Even the machine's friendly name worked against it. Business managers loathed the idea of purchasing a pricey computer with a girl's name. And because it was so complex, software designers had a hard time writing software for it. While Jobs had estimated that Apple would sell 50,000 Lisas in the first year, total sales were less than half that number.

After reengineering and improvements, the Lisa II was introduced. It was later renamed the XL, which insiders joked stood for either "Extra Large" or "Extra Lisas" (for all of the unsold inventory). Jobs, never been one to hesitate, had seen the writing on the wall even before the Lisa II came out: If Apple wanted to create a friendly, interactive computer, it would have to slash the price, and the goodies. Jobs had secretly begun to develop a new machine—one that was smaller, faster, and a third the cost of Lisa. Rumors of this secret computer only hastened Lisa's demise. A year later, Apple management came to the conclusion that the company could not afford to develop both computers. Unwanted and unappreciated, Lisa was abandoned in the spring of 1985 in favor of Jobs's new computer, the Macintosh.

Apple consigned all of its remaining inventory of Lisas to Sun Remarketing of Utah, which refurbished and sold some of them. This ended when Apple decided to take a tax write-off on its unsold inventory. In September 1989, a decade after Jobs had first seen the Alto in action, the last 2,700 Lisas were buried by bulldozer in a Utah landfill, bringing an end to perhaps the greatest and most revolutionary failure in the history of computing, despite being the first mass-marketed computer that virtually all computers to follow would imitate.

You have to admire Apple's bold stroke, even if it wasn't successful. One hallmark of an innovative company is its willingness to swing for the fences, and Apple did just that. As it learned, not every great innovation works, because success is not guaranteed. Yet without the Lisa, there probably would not have been a Macintosh, and in that regard, it is hard to call the Lisa a loser. A commercial success it was not. But important? You bet. So even innovation miscalculation has its place.

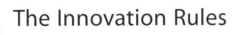

The Innovation Rules

- An undercapitalized innovation can wreak havoc on all concerned.
- Jackals are waiting to steal your idea.
- Unfortunately, innovating well and pricing the product to sell do not always go hand in hand.

!!!!!!!!!!!!!!!!!!!!!!!!!!!

Resistance
Is Futile

Resistance and bureaucracy can come in many forms. It may be a regulatory problem that stands in the way of the innovative idea or it may be middle management, unsure of the changes that may be brought about by a newfangled product. Whatever the case, there are few things more frustrating than facing resistance that threatens to halt the birth of the great new product.

In a large company, facing an internal bureaucratic obstacle is fairly common. Not everyone in the company has the same vision as the business innovator. A new product may be seen as a threat to someone's turf, or the R&D required to get it off the ground may threaten the bottom line. The difference between the bold company and the banal one is that the former demands that its bureaucracy stand aside while the latter is too afraid to change. Alas the poor buggywhip maker, killed by management that couldn't change with the times. One secret to successful business innovation is to avoid the buggywhip syndrome. You do so by creating a corporate culture that welcomes change. You must stand up to bureaucracy in whatever forms it presents and slay it.

A Call to Action
How the Cell Phone Overcame Government Bureaucracy

Remember the 1970s? Of course you remember bell-bottoms, *Saturday Night Fever,* the war in Vietnam, and Donna Summer. But do you remember the state of telecommunications back then? It was a highly regulated industry. AT&T was your long distance carrier. It was the only long distance carrier. If you were on the road and had to make a phone call, you needed a dime and a pay phone. How different was the world back then? If you turned your AM radio tuner to the far end of the band, you might pick up police dispatch calls — there was such a shortage of allotted frequencies that the end of the dial was all that was available for police use. Little did we know, but a much needed telecommunications revolution was on the horizon.

For some time, Motorola had been in the business of creating wireless two-way communication devices. Back then, the technology consisted mostly of walkie-talkies and emergency paging systems. The problem Motorola, among many companies, faced, was that there was not enough bandwidth available to do everything that the engineers could imagine. To expand service, more room was needed in the radio/television spectrum. It was not that there were no wavelengths available, but that they were being reserved by the Federal Communications Commission (FCC). Several companies, including Motorola, petitioned the FCC to open up the lower end of the VHF band (the band where television signals are transmitted). But in the first of several bureaucratic hurdles Motorola had to overcome, the FCC denied the request, stating that when it did open up frequencies they would only be on the high end of the spectrum.

It is important to understand the difference, at the time, between mobile phones and portable phones. Mobile phones were used in cars. Portable phones, what later would be called "cell phones," were not even in existence at the time. The only transportable phone available in the late 1960s was a crude automobile mobile phone system whose use was very limited. In all of Chicago, for example, there were only 2,500 mobile phone numbers available, and most were used by doctors and emergency vehicles. At the time, people shared mobile phone numbers. The phones actually used tubes like an old radio, and the small range that the phones could transmit to, coupled with the fact that users had to manually change frequencies as they traveled across town (sort of like turning the squelch dial on a walkie-talkie), made the system very cumbersome. Yet, according to John F. Mitchell, the Motorola engineer who headed up the company's cell development team, "there was pent-up demand."

Mitchell and his colleagues at Motorola knew that an actual portable cell phone was the answer. By tapping the higher end of the VHF spectrum that was eventually going to be opened up by the FCC, the Motorola team viewed a portable cell phone system, not as a revolutionary innovation but rather as the natural extension of their previous wireless communications work. The engineers at Motorola saw what few others at the time did: By tapping the 900 Mhz frequency and installing cell towers throughout an area, a usable cell phone system could be created that would be able to switch callers from one tower to the next, automatically. So Motorola began to develop cell technology. How visionary was this? Even though there were no cell towers anywhere, even though the FCC had yet to open up the frequencies needed, even though no one even knew what a cell phone was, Mitchell and Motorola knew that cell technology "was where our future lay." Indeed, whatever the challenge, the perceived payoff was worth it. Eventually, Motorola pumped more than $100 million into development of its 900 Mhz technology.

One thing the engineers at Motorola understood was that there were no shortage of radio towers already available. These towers were used for everything from radio broadcasts to police dispatches to a nascent paging system. Adding another frequency to them, a frequency that could be used by portable telephones, "did not seem all that complicated," says Mitchell. He adds that the history of modern electronics meant, "you could forecast, based on the data, that the size, weight, and cost of the eventual cell phone would go down rapidly. We knew that the product would soon be affordable." This point is essential because the first cell phones initially cost $2,500.

Although creating the actual cell technology was not easy, Motorola had a working cell phone by 1973. All that was missing was government licensing. It had taken the company 15 years to take the product from conception to completion, and, says Martin Cooper, a lead engineer on the project, "there were a lot of naysayers over the years." This was even more true within their industry because "AT&T was the industry giant back then and was focused on selling car phones." After working night and day on the project, on April 3, 1973, 97 years after Alexander Graham Bell became the first person ever to speak over a phone ("Mr. Watson, come here. I want to see you."), Martin Cooper became the first person ever to speak over a cell phone. It was then that Cooper lugged his two-pound telephone containing 2,700 different parts to Lexington Avenue in Manhattan and called his friend Joel Engel.

The company obviously had high hopes later that year when the FCC announced that the time had come to open up the high end of the VHF band. Motorola was ready. Sending its best people to Washington, D.C., to testify before Congress and the FCC, Motorola had every reason to believe that the regulatory hurdle before it was simply its latest challenge. Yet, for some reason, be it the times or the lobbyists, the FCC decided to grant an exclusive license to AT&T for its mobile phone business, even though very few, if any, FCC commissioners had ever used a mobile car phone, and none had used a portable cell phone. The folks at Motorola were dumbfounded by what they saw as an amazingly shortsighted decision. But they were out of luck.

Needless to say, panic set in. Motorola had expended too much time, money, and effort on its innovation to let some Washington bureaucrats stand in its way. After a series of emergency meetings, company executives and lawyers came up with a game plan. The only way to beat these thick-headed bureaucrats was to play the game better. This time, they would have a secret weapon. Motorola petitioned the FCC for reconsideration. If you have ever tried to get a regulatory agency to reverse itself, you know the challenge that lay ahead of Motorola. Essentially, it was asking the FCC to admit that it had made a mistake. It is a very rare thing for a regulatory agency to reverse itself in any case, and expecting it to do so, so soon after a decision was made, was practically impossible. But Motorola executives felt like they had little choice, and given that they had a little secret up their sleeve, were reasonably confident that their reconsideration petition just might succeed, or at least make news that day.

Motorola sent its team to the hearing a day or two early to get things ready. Part of the necessary secret apparatus was placed atop a building near where the reconsideration hearing was to take place. On the day of the hearing, a pleasant, if droll, FCC commissioner called the hearing to order. In attendance were several senators, congressmen, AT&T executives, their expensive lobbyists, the people from Motorola (including John Mitchell), and the rest of the FCC commissioners. The FCC commissioner explained that, while Motorola had every right to seek this reconsideration hearing, a decision had been made and the decision was likely final. AT&T's mobile phone technology would set the standard, as AT&T had done so well for so long, and Motorola would have to adapt to the protocols AT&T was creating.

Finally, Mitchell was allowed to speak. He slowly stood up and opened his coat pocket. In his hand was a large, white, boxy-looking phone with a little antenna on top and a mouthpiece at the bottom. It had no wires and was attached to nothing. The commissioners had never seen anything remotely like this contraption. Across the street, atop the neighboring building, the portable cell tower that Motorola engineers had hastily set up the day before powered up and began to emit a silent signal. "Here," Mitchell said to the commissioner, "make a phone call." The commissioner was confused. "How?" So Mitchell demonstrated to the chairman, to the senators and congressman, and to AT&T, what the future would look like. He walked up to the FCC commissioner, showed him how to turn the device on, showed him how to dial and hit "send," and then stood back and waited. Thus, it was here at this reconsideration hearing in 1973 that history was made when the first cell phone call ever in Washington, D.C., took place.

Needless to say, the FCC commissioners were amazed at what Motorola had been able to accomplish. The cell technology it had developed was far superior to the mobile-phone technology the monopolist had created. The FCC reversed its decision and opened up the high end of the VHF band to everyone.

The problems faced by Motorola were not all that unique, especially in such an innovative field as telecommunications. Business is often ahead of government and it is not uncommon that politicians are forced to change rules and regulations to accommodate innovation. What is seen as protection yesterday can become today's suffocation. An altogether different bureaucratic issue arises when it is not some government regulators, but your own company that is intent on stifling your great idea.

The New Volkswagen Beetle
A Friendship Rekindled

If you remember the 1960s, you remember tie-dye clothes, long hair, the Grateful Dead, *The Graduate,* and the war in Vietnam. But do remember cars back then? Most were big gas-guzzlers. Except one. What is the one car that you most associate with that decade? If you are like most people, you would say the Volkswagen (VW) Beetle. Like the times, the Beetle was antiestablishment, and its advertising, with its legendary "think small" campaign, played on the fact that the VW was associated with youth and counterculture. Baby boomers bought the car because it was inexpensive, easy to work on, and a statement against materialism.

By the early 1970s, Volkswagen was selling more than half a million Beetles a year in the United States. (Interesting side note: The word "Beetle" was a nickname that never appeared anywhere on the car.) The car was in movies, on the road, and more popular than ever. But a storm was on the horizon—pending legislation would soon make the car obsolete. The Highway Safety Act of 1966 and the Clean Air Act of 1970, both of which mandated big changes for all autos, highlighted two basic flaws in the Beetle's design: (1) Having a rear engine meant that the car was unsafe in crashes, and (2) being air cooled meant that it couldn't meet upcoming tough emission standards. Rather than completely redesign the car, VW opted out, selling its last Beetle in the United States in 1979.

The death of the Beetle in America lead to an eventual decline of the entire Volkswagen brand in what is the world's largest automobile market. By 1992, sales of all Volkswagens in the United States were an anemic 40,000 units. If something wasn't done soon, VW would soon go the way of other European car manufacturers who had abandoned the lucrative American market, like Renault, Peugeot, and Fiat.

And so a plan was hatched, a plan so secret, so bold, that certainly no one outside VW knew of it, and only three people within the company were aware of it. The genesis for the plan occurred over lunch in 1991. J. Mays, the head of Volkswagen's California design center was meeting with Peter Schreyer, a designer from the German headquarters. The two men were discussing VW's lackluster performance in the United States. They concluded that when people thought of VW, they remembered the Beetle. And their memories of the Beetle were fond indeed. These were the cars of their youth. Many associated freedom and fun with the car. Says Mays, "They didn't necessarily love the car for what it was. They loved what it stood for in their lives."

So Mays left lunch with an idea. What if he could create a new Beetle, a Beetle for the 1990s? Mays called his chief designer, Freeman Thomas, into his office. Mays asked a loaded question, "What do you think of doing a new Beetle?" Thomas loved the idea, figuring that reconceiving the Beetle would inject some much-needed spirit into the moribund company.

But both men knew that the idea was almost too innovative to be a winner, for two reasons. The first was that the Beetle was old news. There was the very real possibility that by bringing the old warhorse back, Volkswagen would essentially be telling people that its best days were behind it. Mays and Freeman knew immediately that the car could not just be retro for the sake of nostalgia. Any new Beetle would have to be a 1990s reinterpretation of the original. Both were confident that this could be done, and in fact, that would be the juice in the project.

The second reason they feared their idea was in trouble was more serious than the first, and definitely more difficult to overcome: their bosses in Germany hated the Beetle. Whereas a couple of designers in California remembered the car fondly, the heads of the company in Germany had an entirely different visceral reaction to the car. They associated the Beetle with Hitler.

Shortly after becoming chancellor of Germany in 1933, Hitler promised that he would build an Autobahn, would reduce taxes on new cars, and would help facilitate the production of a people's car. (In fact, *volks* means people, *wagen* means car, ergo Volkswagen.) In actuality, this was not much of a promise because Hitler knew that such a car was already on the drawing boards of several designers and engineers throughout Europe. Hitler promised a chicken in every pot because he knew there *would* be a chicken in every pot.

Yet many of these designers believed that Hitler had promised too much. The car the Fuehrer called for was small, inexpensive, and very economical to run. In a prelude to the issues faced by the California design team years later, the auto bureaucracy didn't like the car being proposed, didn't think it was feasible, and didn't want it. Faced with auto industry intransigence, Hitler commissioned Dr. Ferdinand Porsche to design the car, and when Hitler commissioned you, it was hard to say no. Even so, several years later, frustrated with Dr. Porsche's foot-dragging, Hitler decided to nationalize the car effort. Funded by the Nazi labor union and its Strength-Through-Joy fund, Hitler decreed that the car would be known as the Strength-Through-Joy car. And so it was that Adolf Hitler conceived of, commissioned, and spearheaded the creation of the people's car, the Strength-Through-Joy mobile, the Volkswagen Beetle.

For that reason, Volkswagen's modern brass wanted nothing to do with a new Beetle, content to leave it to the trash bin of history. J. Mays and Freeman Thomas knew that their biggest battle would not be in redesigning the car but in overcoming the obstinacy of their higher-ups. Says Mays, not so facetiously, "The design only took three days, selling the project took three years." Thomas recalls that "after that first meeting, we sat down and mapped out a plan. People have called us co-conspirators, and I think that's really a good phrase because that is kind of what we were. We were going against the grain and very few people would have agreed with us at that point. So we had to put together a strategy of how to sell the idea and how to fund the idea."

And they did. The first thing they needed was a great design. The key, says Mays, was to "respect what was great about the original Beetle." This meant keeping the same basic shape as the old Beetle while updating and reconceptualizing it. Beginning with drawings and then moving to models as ideas were fleshed out, the two worked in total secret for several years refining their conception of the new old car. Designs were locked away, meetings were held in private, and clay models were photographed in secret locales, all so that they could present the idea when they thought they would have the best chance to change some minds.

By 1993, with a design that they were very happy with, Mays and Thomas felt ready to take on the Volkswagen bureaucracy. Though their boss Harmut Warkuss knew of their dabbling, getting him and Volkswagen to agree to create a full-scale model and concept car was another story altogether. But Thomas and Mays understood that Warkuss was the key to the kingdom. He was the fulcrum that could lift all Volkswagen. If they could get him, they could get the car.

So instead of simply showing their boss their models, Mays and Thomas knew that they had to do something more to overcome inertia. If they simply showed Warkuss their concept, he might like it or and he might not. What they felt they had to do was to create a positive emotional reaction to the car. If they could get him to associate the new car with their California vision of the old Bug, and not his preconceived negative memory, their chances of success would increase dramatically. They needed to evoke a positive and dramatic feeling in him. But how? After several options were rejected, Mays and Thomas finally hit upon one that they hoped would work. If it did not, their dream, and two years' worth of work, would go down the drain. So they concocted a plan.

A short while later, their props ready and their plan set, they invited Warkuss to a conference room and asked him to sit down. The lights dimmed. Warkuss was confused. Soon, a projection screen lit up. Soft music filtered into the room, and before long, a full-blown multimedia presentation was underway. Using slides, voice-overs, and music, Mays and Thomas set about creating a mood. Like a film director tugging at the heartstrings, the auto designers had created a multimedia presentation intended to hit their boss in the gut, and then, hopefully, his head.

The high-tech presentation nostalgically harkened back to 1949 when VW only sold two cars in the United States. The music jumped and the slides segued into the company's apex in the mid-1970s. The music became moody as the then-current sad state of affairs was examined. The room grew dark. But there was hope! Innovation was the way out! Slides of the new Beetle models (cue the soaring musical score!) and an explanation of what the new car could be filled the room. The past was not just the past, *the past was prologue.* A new Beetle could be a reaffirmation of the best that Volkswagen had to offer—honesty, simplicity, reliability, originality. Nothing less than the soul of the company was at stake.

When the show was over, Warkuss stood up, looked at the two men, and rapped his knuckles on the desk, the German equivalent of a standing ovation. Says Mays, "That meeting was the turning point. It touched him. We knew then that the car was an emotional fireball." Warkuss was taken to the designers' studio and shown the models. Now in the right frame of mind, he loved the car and ordered that the multimedia presentation be shipped to his cohorts in Germany. Though they were clearly reluctant to broach the issue, the German hierarchy also knew that the company needed a boost. They too saw that the inspired design was something special. Says Rudiger Folten, a design team leader, "We had been making Golfs for 20 years. We were distant from the Beetle. The Beetle was part of our history and nearly forgotten. In California, the Beetle was still alive, and the designers could see that." The brass at Volkswagen couldn't help but see it too. Within a few months, as Mays and Thomas had hoped, management had fallen in line and agreed to the project, proving that a great idea can sometimes trump a stubborn belief.

From there, things moved quickly. The concept car, known as Concept 1, was the undisputed hit of the 1994 International Car Show in Detroit. The announcer introduced Concept 1, stating, "It's funny the things we remember, the things we hang onto. The first day of school. A first dance. A first kiss. Our first car. Some things are simply unforgettable. What if quality never went out of style? What if originality still meant something original? Imagine a new Volkswagen. An expression of innovation. One look, and it all comes back. The legend reborn. A friendship rekindled."

And indeed a friendship was rekindled. The New Beetle became not just a hit, but a cultural phenomenon. Dealers in North America were allegedly selling the car for $4,000 over the sticker price. Overall Volkswagen sales jumped 50 percent. One wonders what could top the astounding success of the New Beetle. A revived VW Microbus? Says Free-man Thomas coyly, "What about it?" Well, why not? Having revived the dead once, who is to say he and Mays can't do it again?

An inventor who faces bureaucratic hurdles is dou-bly vexed: Not only must he figure out how to create the next great thing, but he must simultaneously finesse his way through the establishment. The innovator, by his or her very nature, is iconoclastic, independent, usually noncon-formist, and looking to shake things up, while the nature of a bureaucracy is to maintain the status quo and keep things on a steady course. When the innovative irresistible force hits the bureaucratic immovable object, something has to give, and it is not always the establishment. To keep the innovation alive requires political skills on top of technical and business savvy. This is even more true when the estab-lished order doesn't understand what the innovator is doing, or, worse, is dead-set opposed to it. Such was the sit-uation during the 1960s, when a genius named Douglas Engelbart helped create a product that changed the world, something you probably use every day.

The Big Cheese
The Man Behind the Computer Mouse

Who is Douglas Engelbart and why have you never heard of him? Good question, because by all rights, you should have. Unlike most innovators in this book, he is not a business-man or an unfettered capitalist, but rather a visionary sci-entist devoted to improving the lot of humanity.

The futurist grew up in an idyllic setting on a one-acre farm near Portland, Oregon, during the Depression, before going off to study electrical engineering at Oregon State University. He spent two years in the Navy at the end of World War II, where his early experiences would help to shape his later results. As an electronics technician in the Philippines, he worked with radar, where he learned that information could be displayed and manipulated on a screen. After the war, he received a bachelor's degree from Oregon State University in 1948, and then settled, seemingly contentedly, on the San Francisco peninsula as an electrical engineer at NACA Ames Laboratory (the forerunner of NASA).

However, within three years, Engelbart grew restless, feeling there was something more important he should be working on, dedicating his career to. "I looked downstream at work [and saw] one long, uneventful hallway," he recalls. "I had no proper goals that interested me." He realized that he had been given "5½ million minutes" before he was 65. How could those minutes best be used? His conclusion: "Why don't I try to maximize the value of my career in the sense of how to benefit mankind?" he remembers. "Can you imagine that?" he asks. "To this day I don't know where that came from."

What did this mean in practical terms? Then, as now, money was not one of his main concerns. He asked himself, "'What are my [financial] requirements?' Well, I could earn a lot of money, but I hadn't yet had any perception of what money was worth. I finally said, 'Well, let's just put as a requirement—I'll get enough out of it to live reasonably well.'" Of far greater importance, Engelbart decided, was his ability to maximize the use of his time. "I started poking around, looking at the different kinds of crusades I could get in on. I soon realized that if I wanted to contribute in some maximum way, I'd need to provide some real driving force, because to just go be a soldier in somebody else's crusade was not a way to be satisfied."

What really began to interest him, indeed what became his driving force, was an understanding that life was becoming more and more complex, and man's ability to solve problems was becoming correspondingly more difficult. "It suddenly flashed that if you could do something to improve human capability to deal with that, then you'd really contribute something basic. That just resonated. Then it unfolded rapidly." The *it* that unfolded was as noteworthy for its daring as its vision. Engelbart says that within an hour he had a vision of a screen with all kinds of symbols on it. The amazing thing about this vision was that, at the time in the early 1950s, computers were gigantic machines that were used primarily for number crunching and had no screens at all, and Douglas Engelbart knew nothing about computers. Even so, he saw a future where the computer could be an interactive tool, operated by "any kind of a lever or knob, or buttons, or switches, you wanted." Engelbart understood in that flash of inspiration that a computer might eventually be able to sense these peripheral devices and respond to them. "That gave me a goal," he says.

"I literally, at that time, didn't know how the computer worked," he readily admits. Yet, despite that, as his epiphany continued, "I also really got a clear picture that one's colleagues could be sitting in other rooms with similar work stations, tied to the same computer complex, and could be sharing and working and collaborating very closely." Within a matter of hours, he realized that this was the crusade he had been searching for, and knew as well that he would need to hook up with a university that was working with computers. He looked for a place to get a Ph.D., found there was no such thing as a computer science department at any school, and settled on the University of California at Berkeley, a school that was building an experimental computer. In 1955, he got his doctorate.

After graduation, Dr. Engelbart accepted a research position at the Stanford Research Institute (SRI, now the Stanford Research Laboratory), where he earned a dozen patents in two years. By 1959, he had enough standing to get approval to pursue his own research. He then spent the next two years turning his computer vision into a theoretical framework. In 1962, Dr. Engelbart published a landmark paper outlining his vision. In 132 pages, "Augmenting Human Intellect: A Conceptual Framework" laid a path toward much of what has happened to this day in computers. In it, he envisioned what you see on your computer today. His proposed project, as outlined in the report, was big, calling for software creation, hardware invention, and user interface; none of which had even been contemplated, let alone invented. By 1963, he procured enough funding to start his own research lab within SRI, which he later dubbed the Augmentation Research Center (ARC). Engelbart assembled a team, and together they began to research the kinds of computer technology he believed would be required to augment our human intellect.

At the time, a computer was made with vacuum tubes. It filled a room. It got instructions from punched cards. It spat out data. The idea that a computer could be tied to a display screen and that images on this screen could somehow be manipulated was heresy. Indeed, the so-called "direct manipulation interface," where visible objects on the screen are directly manipulated with a pointing device, would not become commonplace for almost 20 years, when Apple introduced the first Macintosh in 1984. In the 1960s though, computers were still big, lumbering data crunchers, and ARC was venturing into uncharted waters.

The areas that the team at ARC was delving into, things like computer interactivity and graphic manipulation of screens, were areas that no one else cared about. "It was so hard to find people to take us seriously when computers were so big and expensive," Engelbart recalls. "But I realized that inevitably they would get smaller and smaller, and faster and faster, and cheaper and cheaper. I realized that might happen in my lifetime." But no one else did, and Engelbart's battle against bureaucracy began. SRI was a conservative institution and Engelbart, with his penchant for saving humanity and his odd choice of research, was a maverick—not a good combination.

Nevertheless, in the beginning, ARC had unfettered opportunities to conduct its research, and it did so by starting from scratch. Engelbart recalls, "This is how crude it was: There wasn't anything like a disk. We didn't have magnetic tape until somewhat later. So the only input/output storage medium was paper tape. If you started editing something, when you were ready to quit, you would punch it out, and wind it up. When you were ready to go back to work, you would first load the parent program and take the tape and it would load your text to start working on it. If it crashed, we'd have to go back and start all over again." Despite this, the scientists at ARC began to forge a vision of how computers could be used to increase human intelligence. They wanted to craft a set of tools that could enable people and organizations to harness what they saw as the incredible power of computers.

It was at a graphics conference where the inspiration for a computer-pointing device first came to Engelbart. "I carried little notebooks around for years. They were carried in my front shirt pocket and I would get thinking about things and I'd have a place to write them." He recalls sitting at the graphics conference and wondering how the curser on a screen might be controlled in a different way. He got to thinking about a device from his engineering days, "a little, simple mechanical thing." This rolling tool had a bent arm and a little disc that rode at the end. When one part of the mechanism rolled, the disc at the other end followed the same path. Engelbart explains that "if you have a little wheel and you push it this far . . . it essentially doesn't matter what path you follow between those two spots. It will roll the same no matter what." He says, "I just got to thinking about those two wheels. Soon the rest of it was very simple, so I went and made a sketch."

From that sketch, the researchers at ARC created the very first computer mouse. Made from a wood block, the tool, Engelbart says, was fairly simple to devise. Going from moving a mouse on a pad to moving a cursor on a screen was, he says, actually quite easy, "The thing of taking an analog voltage and converting it to digital has been a basic instrumentation device from way, way back; and that's all that it was." They put three buttons at one end because "that was all there was room for." They named it a mouse because that's what it looked like, although no one can remember who first came up with the name. Engelbart recalls, "You know, I can say, 'This thing we built, called the mouse—it just happened.'" He received a patent for the wooden shell with two metal wheels in 1970, describing it in the patent application as an "X-Y position indicator for a display system."

But at the same time, while things were going swimmingly in the lab, all was not well outside its four walls. Engelbart notes that his superiors at SRI "were really fairly troubled about me and what I wanted to do." He had been passed up at least once for a review; they were trying to decide whether to fire him, an uncommon occurrence at SRI. "They just thought I was way too far out." SRI decided that it would be better for all involved if Engelbart concentrated on being behind the scenes, writing proposals or some such thing. The problem with him was that instead of working within the existing framework at SRI, Engelbart had decided to create a different framework for his explorations and "work within that, until my work was recognized as a different kind of area." As a result, there was created around Engelbart and his ARC "a sort of negative aura about stubborn, uncooperative me and my lab. I just got a hopeless feeling about trying to communicate to any of them what was different in what I was trying to do."

Something dramatic would have to happen if Engelbart and ARC were to stay in existence, let alone create a tool that could make life a little less complex. "Looking around the Institute, I had some good friends who were very concerned personally, but who didn't seem to know what to do [for me]." Because interactive computers were something out of a Buck Rogers story at the time, very few people understood the importance of what was going on inside ARC. So when SRI managers asked different people about the lab, the answer invariably was, "Well, they're off on cloud nine over there at ARC," observed Engelbart.

To make matters worse, not only was he pegged as a "blue sky" kind of guy, but his budget became a problem as well. Funding is often a source of concern for research laboratories, and finding the funding to keep his cutting-edge research alive was becoming increasingly difficult, especially without the backing of his superiors. Engelbart recalls, "It was just unbearable. I tried to figure where I could go and what I could do. I thought of going to MIT or somewhere. It was miserable." In the midst of this, a fortuitous phone call came from NASA. They were looking into similar research and offered ARC $80,000. It wasn't enough to do everything Engelbart envisioned, but it was enough to keep the dream alive.

By 1968, Engelbart says, "I was beginning to feel that we could show a lot of dramatic things. Maybe what we needed to do was to show a lot of people at once. I got the picture of what we could potentially do." In March of that year, he learned that the Joint Computer Conference was going to be held at the Convention Center in San Francisco that December. Engelbart thought that if he could put on a live demonstration of what ARC had created to date, he might attract enough attention to take his research to the next level. So he called the conference promoters and offered to put on a live demonstration of just what a computer could actually do. But the people putting on the conference were very hesitant. Twice they sent people to ARC to see what Engelbart and his colleagues were doing. So revolutionary was ARC's work that even those who were putting together the computer conference didn't understand it. Remember, the first commercially viable mass-market computer, the Apple II, would not even be released for another ten years.

The demonstration was a huge gamble. Not only was the team at ARC not sure that they could pull it off, but they knew that if they blew it, it would hurt their own prospects, and the reputation of their financial backers. Engelbart remembers being concerned about NASA. "I knew that if it really crashed or if somebody really complained [using government money to put on the presentation], there could be enough trouble that it could blow the whole program; they would have to cut me off and blackball us."

Yet despite the considerable risk, Engelbart also knew that they needed to do something dramatic to take the bureaucratic heat off and capture people's imaginations. Engelbart decided to do the live demonstration with a colleague at ARC in Palo Alto, participating remotely to boot. The first thing they needed was a video projector, which, back then, was not a common piece of equipment. They were able to rent one, says Engelbart, from "some outfit in New York. They had to fly it out and a man to run it." A platform was built for Engelbart, where he would sit with a keyboard in the middle, a wooden mouse on his right, and a set of "F keys" on his left. This demonstration was so important, so unprecedented, "so much swung on it," that Engelbart was "nervous as hell." It would take a lot of special technology, and no small amount of luck, to get everything to work properly and pull it off. Just in case, ARC decided to have some trial presentations captured on film to use as a backup.

On December 9, 1968, Douglas C. Engelbart and the group of 17 researchers working with him in the Augmentation Research Center at Stanford Research Institute, presented the first-ever live public demonstration of the online system they had been working on since 1962. About 1,000 computer professionals attended the public presentation. For 90 minutes, Dr. Engelbart used his mouse to manipulate text and pictures on a giant screen. He reorganized a grocery list, communicated with coworkers at SRI in Menlo Park, 35 miles away, and put their pictures on the screen. Pointers from each man's mouse flicked around the screen as they jointly revised a document. Not only was this the public debut of the computer mouse, but it was also the first-ever public demonstration of many computer tools we now take for granted, including text editing, integration of text and graphics, shared-screen teleconferencing, and technology that allowed people to collaborate on problems from different locations.

Engelbart received a standing ovation. The demonstration turned out to be a landmark event. Like Woodstock or Wilt Chamberlain's 100-point game, this was one of those times when many more people than actually attended said they were there. "I keep being surprised when I run across people who really were there," chuckles Engelbart. For his part, Douglas Engelbart was happy that nothing crashed. "I was so relieved. So many things could have broken," he says, recalling the jury-rigged setup and the antennas carrying the message from Menlo Park to a truck with antennas that connected to a roof in San Francisco. But he also notes that he never had to worry about funding again. (If you would like to see Englebart's demonstration for yourself, you can.

It is available online for viewing at <http://sloan.stanford .edu/mousesite/1968Demo.html>.)

It is now said that this famous demonstration launched the computer revolution. For the first time, a mass of people began to realize what computers could actually do. "It was stunning," says Bob Taylor, who won the 1999 Medal of Technology for his contributions to developing personal computers and the Internet. "It really woke a lot of people up to a whole new way of thinking about computers—not just as number crunches." Says futurist Paul Saffo of Menlo Park's Institute for the Future, "Doug Engelbart stands as the single most misunderstood pioneer in the history of computing. His ideas are still ahead of their time." But Patrick Lincoln, the head of computer science at SRI, says that Engelbart is "outdated." Says Lincoln, "He's a thousand years ahead of his time."

It is a fact: When you try to do something extraordinary, revolutionary, both the risks and the rewards are great. If it works, you are likely to grow old very rich, satisfied that you made a difference, and content that you were unique. If it doesn't, you could end up broke, resentful, sad, or all of these. There are no guarantees in this life, and rejection is just as likely, maybe even more likely, a result of innovative efforts as success. One reason for this is that resistance usually meets innovation head on. But resistance need not prevail. A groundbreaking product can still succeed, in spite of whatever forces are teamed against it. What is needed is persistence, commitment, and belief.

Battling Depression
Resisting the Opposition to Prozac

In 1972, Democratic vice presidential nominee Thomas Egleton was so stigmatized and marginalized by his previous bouts with depression, and his efforts to deal with it, that he hid these facts from presidential nominee George McGovern when he was looking at potential running mates. When it later came out during the campaign that Egleton had indeed suffered from depression and had undergone shock-treatment therapy for it, the ensuing uproar forced Egleton from the race.

Egleton is certainly not alone in suffering from depression. It is estimated that during the course of a year, 17.5 million Americans suffer from clinical depression. One in 5 women will suffer from major depression at some time in her life, as will 1 in 15 men. Someone who has just one episode of major depression also has a 50-50 chance of more episodes, perhaps as many as one or two a year. More than 18,000 people commit suicide each year, as a result of depression.

Says *60 Minutes* correspondent Mike Wallace, "I cannot tell you how painful depression is. I have never known agony like it, and I'm an old man." Abraham Lincoln, who struggled with depression much of his adult life, once said, "I am now the most miserable man living. If what I feel were equally distributed to the whole human family, there would be not one cheerful face on earth. Whether I shall ever be better, I cannot tell. I awfully forebode I shall not." Like all depression sufferers, President Lincoln wanted help, but saw no way out of his black hole. Indeed, prior to the development and introduction of Prozac, depression was a debilitating, misunderstood disease. No one would ever say that a heart attack could be prevented if only the patient would just "snap out of it," but that is precisely the sort of attitude faced by depression sufferers for many years.

Before the advent of the current crop of antidepressants, known collectively as selective serotonin reuptake inhibitors (SSRIs), therapies offered to the depressed basically boiled down to three types: electroconvulsive shock therapy, counseling, and pharmaceuticals. Although not as gruesome as depicted in movies, shock therapy is not a pleasant experience. Electricity shot though the brain can sideline a bout of depression, but proves usually to be a temporary measure. It may not cure the disease, and often it destroys parts of the memory. Similarly, various forms of talking therapy—in- cluding behavioral therapy, cognitive therapy, and psychodynamic therapy—are mostly ineffective in curing the underlying biochemical upset that causes endogenous depression. In the pharmaceutical arena, doctors have tried everything from stimulants, such as amphetamines, to lithium and iproniazide, all without great results. The problem with these drugs was that they didn't always work, and often had severe side effects. These earlier antidepressants also required weeks of experimentation to arrive at a correct dosage. Patients were required to take a little medicine each day, then build up the dosage to find the amount that was right for them, and even then, these drugs simply didn't work all that well for many people.

Scientists have long known that clinical depression is a neurotransmitter problem. What they didn't know was how to create a drug that targeted the specific neurotransmitters in question without affecting other ones. It is akin to living in a home and having a light bulb burn out. You wouldn't call in an electrician to rip out all the wiring in the walls, you would just replace the bulb. It's the same way with depression. If you have a malfunction in one neurotransmitter system, there is really no need to take a drug that will interfere with other neurotransmitter systems and receptor sites throughout your brain. But, for many years, antidepressant drugs did just that because no one knew how to design a drug that would hone in on the light bulb—the serotonin—and ignore the wiring in the rest of the house.

Neurotransmitters are chemicals that carry messages between nerve cells. They are secreted by one cell and picked up by receptor proteins on the surface of another. Once the message has been delivered, a neurotransmitter is either destroyed or retrieved into the cell that made it. This process is known as reuptake. When reuptake is inhibited, the effect of the serotonin is amplified, and when serotonin is amplified, depression is reduced. The problem was that scientists had been unable to create a drug that specifically targeted serotonin levels. For years, scientists searched for this miracle drug, looking at different models of nerve transmission and tailoring chemicals to affect these basic processes.

Among those who tried to solve this problem were researchers at Eli Lilly, the giant pharmaceutical company. Beginning in the 1960s, when Lilly chemists began examining serotonin pathways, and on through the 1970s when they began to look at chemical causes of depression, its creation of Prozac was more a planned evolution than a surprise discovery. Lilly put tremendous efforts behind solving the serotonin riddle, spending untold millions over the course of 20 years, knowing that potentially huge profits lay waiting for the company that could devise a better antidepressant. The breakthrough finally came in 1974, when David Wong and Bryan Molloy discovered that one of the compounds they had been working with, labeled 82816, blocked the uptake of serotonin and very little else in laboratory rats. Compound 82816 was found to be 200 times more active in inhibiting serotonin than any other known drug. 82816 was fluoxetine hydrochloride, and fluoxetine hydrochloride is Prozac.

The company had very high hopes for Prozac. For the first time, doctors would have a way to replace a burned-out bulb without rewiring the whole house. Unlike the shotgun approach of older drugs, Prozac and other SSRIs zero in on serotonin without affecting other brain systems. Moreover, its relative lack of side effects would allow Prozac to be used freely. This meant that it would likely interfere less than other drugs with the psychoanalytic relationship. And because of its reduced negative effects on the heart, doctors could prescribe it to potentially suicidal patients.

Within only a few months, the reviews were in and they were rave. Patients loved Prozac. With Prozac, patients were able to feel "normal" again. Many people who had suffered from depression for years reported that they hadn't felt so good in a long time. Doctors reported that they were finally able to treat patients who, for a variety of reasons, were heretofore untreatable. In 1988, only months after it was approved and distributed, prescriptions reached over 2.5 million, more than any other antidepressant.

As a result, the introduction of Prozac created the sort of media buzz that is usually reserved for presidential scandals and celebrity peccadilloes. By the spring of 1990, Prozac had made the covers of both the *New Yorker* and *Newsweek,* touted as the "new wonder drug for depression." The name *Prozac* soon became a household word, and there was no escaping its fame. Success stories could be seen on every talk show, and Prozac had established itself as the miracle drug that scientists had long searched for. By 1992, prescriptions had reached 9.6 million, double the amount of its closest competitor. In 1993, Prozac gained even more recognition when psychiatrist Peter Kramer wrote *Listening to Prozac,* which spent 21 weeks on the *New York Times* bestseller list. According to Lilly, 35 million patients to date throughout the world have been prescribed Prozac.

Prozac revolutionized the treatment of clinical depression, and has had a dramatic effect on the public's misperception of the disease—moving the illness from stigma to public understanding and acceptance. "Prozac ushered in a new era of antidepressant treatment," says Dr. David S. Goldbloom, Physician-in-Chief at the Center for Addiction and Mental Health at the University of Toronto. "It has been associated with a decrease in stigma around the illness, an increase in recognition of depression, and a simplicity in use." As patients were treated with a simple and straightforward medicine by their family doctors, and without noticeable side effects, the notion that it was acceptable to be "depressed" grew. Prozac became an icon symbolizing the growing destigmatization of mental illness. "The extraordinary public attention and success of Prozac has helped to focus attention on mood disorders generally, and has encouraged millions of people to reach out and get help for these very treatable disorders," says Dr. Frederick Paulson, a noted Prozac expert.

Unfortunately for Eli Lilly, the Prozac story does not end here. A few years after the introduction of its new drug, the company began to hear unanticipated criticisms of Prozac, resulting in challenges and resistance that it hadn't planned on. Scientists initially thought that the side effects of taking Prozac could include anxiety, nervousness, insomnia, sweating, drowsiness, fatigue, dizziness, nausea, loss of appetite, or diarrhea. Compared to severe depression, these side effects were not a problem for most people. For a few patients, however, the miracle drug turned out to be a disaster with side effects that no one warned them about. For a small, select group of users, Prozac actually increased depressive symptoms. These depressed people allegedly became suicidal while on the drug.

Within a few years of its introduction, reports of adverse side effects from Prozac started to make news as well. By the end of 1993, a total of 28,623 complaints of adverse side effects had been filed with the FDA, including 1,885 suicide attempts and 1,349 deaths allegedly attributable to taking Prozac. A group of highly vocal dissidents arose in protest of Prozac. They were buttressed in 1994, when David Healy, then a consultant to Eli Lilly, published an article entitled "The Fluoxetine and Suicide Controversy, a Review of the Evidence." In that paper, Healy opined that antidepressants, Prozac included, can indeed induce suicidal behavior in a minority of patients. In 2000, the book *Prozac Backlash* was published.

Not every breakthrough product will be met by a grateful, willing public. Resistance can come in many forms. This is especially true in the pharmaceutical arena, where side effects are expected. Yet, resistance must be dealt with if the product is to survive and thrive. Lilly responded to mounting criticism by taking the high road. It points out that in the vast majority of cases, Prozac has been a godsend. For every negatively effected user, there are a hundred who gladly take their Prozac every day. And it is hard to argue with that analysis. The safety and effectiveness of Prozac has certainly been thoroughly studied in clinical trials with more than 35,000 patients. More than 6,000 scientific papers have been published that discuss the safety and effectiveness of Prozac, the vast majority concluding the drug is usually very safe. Lilly also points out that the FDA continues to approve Prozac for a wide variety of mental illnesses, and that the regulatory agency would not do that if Prozac were not safe. In 1994, for example, Prozac received FDA approval to be marketed for the treatment of obsessive-compulsive disorder, and in 1996, Prozac became the first medication to receive FDA approval for the treatment of bulimia.

For all the criticism, the fact is Prozac has been generally considered a breakthrough drug. In 1999, two Lilly scientists who had significant roles in the discovery of fluoxetine hydrochloride—the active compound in Prozac—were recognized by the U.S. Department of Commerce, receiving the prestigious American Innovator Award. The award is an annual recognition presented to inventors whose products have produced important contributions to society. Bryan B. Molloy and Klaus Schmiegel, the two Lilly scientists credited with inventing Prozac (although hundreds were actually involved), were inducted into the National Inventors Hall of Fame that same year. Says August M. Watanabe, executive vice president of science and technology at Lilly, "Prozac opened the door to a better way of treating depression and remains, to this day, the most commonly used antidepressant in history." Says Molloy, "Prozac has had an important role not only in the treatment of depression, but also in the destigmatization of mental illness. Making such a invention is always a thrill for a scientist. The fact that Prozac has had a crucial role in millions of lives makes the discovery even more meaningful."

And from a business perspective, maybe the most significant award for Prozac was bestowed upon it on November 22, 1999, when it was called by *Fortune* magazine one of the top "Products of the Century."

The Innovation Rules

- Expect resistance.
- Bureaucracy is intended to maintain the status quo, so don't expect it to fall easily.
- Publicity is a great way to usurp authority.

!!!!!!!!!!!!!!!!!!!!!!!!!!!

Patience Is a Virtue

Patience and *innovation* are words that seem diametrically opposed to one another. Patience is plodding. Patience is structured. Patience demands hard work and self-discipline. It is drab and unglamorous. Patience is, well, patient. Innovation on the other hand is exciting! It is new and different and fun. It is cutting edge. It is revolution. By its very nature, innovation is in a hurry, as it must not lose the inherent advantage that comes with being first. Innovation that is second is imitation. So innovation must be ahead of the curve.

Yet it is not always possible to be innovative and quick at the same time. Sometimes it is impossible, for myriad reasons, to swiftly turn your idea into a product and then into dollars. Indeed, the very nature of turning a thought into a thing requires time. Ideally, the "eureka!" idea can be materialized in short order, but when it can't be, the maker of that product faces the very real prospect that his or her baby will be moot.

So the persistent innovator is almost an oxymoron. Almost. For you see, it is this individual alone, among all the innovators, who is the one who may be the most committed, the one who simply cannot let the idea die. He or she continues to hold onto it, in spite of obstacles. A select few are able to continue on, through the years, patiently plodding on and holding steady to their vision in spite of the slings and arrows of outrageous fortune. Eventually, they get their product to market.

They do so through a combination of plucky determinism, inherent faith in their vision, hard work, and plain, old-fashioned stubbornness. These innovators prove that, while getting a great innovative idea to market is no easy task, neither is it impossible. Consider the long-awaited, much-delayed, oft-ridiculed, one and only, Barbie.

Worth the Wait
Barbie's Long Road to the Prom

To understand the patience that it took to bring Barbie to market, it is important to know up front that Barbie was first conceived of in 1951 but didn't make it to the New York Toy Show until 1959. Even though almost a decade would intervene between conception and fruition, Barbie was still an amazingly innovative product. To begin with, she was the first doll for girls that was a woman and not a girl. At the time, the conventional wisdom was that girls liked to play mommy and, as such, dolls were made to be babies and little kids. Barbie, by being a woman, turned conventional wisdom on its head. The woman who conceived of Barbie was Mattel cofounder Ruth Handler. She had long wanted Mattel to create a woman doll, but was told time and again that the product was both unfeasible and unmarketable. Says Ms. Handler, "That was the *official* reason my idea was rejected. But I really think that the squeamishness of those designers, every last one of them male, stemmed mostly from the fact that the doll would have breasts." And that was the second thing that made Barbie so innovative—her breasts.

Ruth Handler knew, from her own experience, that girls wanted to be more than mommies when they played. In the 1950s, toy stores sold a lot of paper dolls. Ruth noticed that her daughter Barbara (also called Barbie) and her friends preferred to play with the adult female paper dolls. "They were simply not interested in baby paper dolls," she says. As Ms. Handler listened to her daughter and her friends play with the dolls, she "discovered something very important: They were using these dolls to project their dreams of their own futures as adult women. It dawned on me that this was a basic, much needed play pattern that had never before been offered by the doll industry to little girls."

That is exactly the kind of opening that the innovative mind looks for: An untapped need waiting to be filled. Handler's insight was that "through the doll, the little girl could be anything she wanted to be." So she spoke with her husband and cofounder Elliot, and with the toy designers. "They all looked at me blankly." Her idea was so new, so innovative, that others couldn't see what she saw. Years went by, and Ruth continued to bring up the idea, but no one at the company was interested. No one had ever made such a doll before, or so they thought until a fateful day in France.

Ruth, Elliot, and their two children (the aforementioned Barbie, and her brother—you guessed it—Ken) were in Lucerne five years later. Standing outside a toy store, Ms. Handler was "transfixed by the window display." There in front of her was the doll she had envisioned so many years earlier. Here were six "Lilli" dolls: Small waist, long hair, tapered legs, and . . . breasts! Though even more voluptuous than Barbie turned out to be, there were the adult-style dolls Ruth had dreamed about, wearing interchangeable fashionable European ski clothes to boot.

Ruth showed the doll to her husband and business partner, Elliot. Finally, after all these years, he understood what she had been talking about and agreed that the idea was definitely worth pursuing. So Ruth bought a few Lillis, packed them well, and brought them back to Mattel's research and design department in Los Angeles. The head of R&D for Mattel, Jack Ryan, was just heading to Japan on business when Ruth Handler caught up with him. Before he left, Handler sat down with him and showed Ryan the dolls. She explained that this is what she had been talking about and that she and Elliot wanted to explore the possibility of creating a similar doll for the Mattel line. She told Ryan that while he was in Japan, he should try to find someone who could manufacture a doll similar to Lilli.

Bringing an innovative product to market is usually difficult, but Barbie was exceptionally so. At the time Mattel agreed to green-light the project, it did not realize that manufacturing Barbie would be quite so challenging. Aside from the need to find a cost-effective production method, Mattel had to develop a slew of new manufacturing techniques. As is often the case in business, the road you head down sometimes veers off in an unexpected direction. To get back to where you were originally headed, your choice is often to allocate the necessary resources and forge ahead. That is what Mattel ended up doing after committing to manufacture the new doll. Rather than take no for an answer, the company remained committed to Ruth's vision and found a way to create the new product.

After an exhaustive search, Ryan finally located the only Japanese manufacturer with the potential for producing the doll. Kokusai Boeki had the sort of "rotational casting" capabilities that the new doll would require. Mattel and Boeki struck a deal that would soon make "made in Japan" part of the American lexicon. Once it had a manufacturer, Mattel had to figure out how, exactly, the doll would be made. The

Lilli doll was made of hard plastic. Handler says that she wanted "a friendlier, softer material." But soft and plastic are not words that usually go together. Mattel researchers tried a variety of synthetic materials, but none were quite right. The company finally settled on vinyl, but having little experience using vinyl to create a toy, Mattel had to find outside help. It turned to B.F. Goodrich to figure out how vinyl could be used in rotational casting.

Barbie would eventually become as well-known for her hair as for her measurements, but creating those flowing locks was problematic from the start. It took months to find a material that seemed realistic enough to pass for hair, yet sturdy enough to hold up to child's play. At the time, almost all dolls had a hairline painted on the tops of their heads; actual tresses were rare. Even after Mattel found a synthetic material that would work, figuring out how to attach it to the doll's tiny head became more of an issue. Glue would not work because Mattel expected that the doll would be played with fairly roughly and it didn't want her hair falling out. The logical answer, to sew the hair on, proved almost impossible because there were seemingly no sewing machines available that could perform the nimble work. It took yet another exhaustive search to find a machine for the job. Even then, it was such a delicate job that training people to do the rooting without accidentally sewing hair in her eye or ear took time as well. Finally, Mattel developed a method of painting the scalp the same color as the hair. This served as a guideline so that the women who did the rooting could shape Barbie's hairline.

Early on in this laborious process, Mattel hired a professional clothing designer to design a wardrobe for Barbie. Charlotte Johnson taught at the Chouinard Art School and agreed to moonlight as Barbie's clothing designer. Soon after the project began, she came to work full-time at Mattel but quickly ran into production problems of her own. The printed fabric that was available for her to work with had patterns that were simply too big in scale to use on such a small doll body—the flowers on a flowered Barbie dress had to be the size of tack. Handler realized that they would have to design their own fabrics if Barbie was to ever make it to market. The clothes that Charlotte Johnson eventually designed were unlike anything the toy industry had seen before: tiny hems, zippers, snaps, piping, buttons, and buttonholes. The clothes were made in Japan because, according to Handler, "Japanese women, with their smaller hands and traditionally more nimble fingers, were ideally suited for making these tiny garments."

It took three years to make a Barbie from a Lilli, and along the way, Mattel was forced to invent all sorts of new processes and inventions. Finally, however, in 1959, Barbie was ready for the prom, or what the toy industry commonly refers to as the Toy Show. Held in New York City every year, the Toy Show is the industry showcase for toy manufacturers, with more than 1,600 manufacturers, 2,000 showrooms, and 16,000 buyers. With a suggested retail price of $3, Barbie came to the show ready for her close-up. But no one else was. Response to the peculiar new doll was mixed at best. The *New York Times* business section story on the show buried Barbie on the inside of the section, several paragraphs down, dismissing her as Mattel's attempt to "balance the heavy male emphasis on toy guns."

The response of the industry to Barbie's rollout was so dismal that Mattel faced the very real possibility that it had bet on the wrong horse. With the now-functioning production facilities in Japan churning out 20,000 dolls and 40,000 outfits a month, the company verged on having a very real crisis of unsold inventory and worthless cash projections. Who said innovation would be rewarded?

The public, that's who. While the toy industry was lukewarm to the radical new doll, girls, as we all now know, simply loved Barbie. The few stores that bought initial shipments sold out very quickly. Says Ken Handler, "The reorders began crashing through the doors, pouring out of mailboxes, oozing under the woodwork, and through the air-conditioning ducts." Stores that didn't order her the first time lined up for round two. Production in Japan was immediately doubled. In short order, Ruth Handler's dream had become Mattel's runaway hit. The company simply could not make Barbie dolls fast enough to meet the deluge that was rapidly developing.

Not only did sales of the innovative product exceed all expectations, but Barbie immediately became a cultural phenomenon. Within two years of her introduction, Barbie was receiving in excess of 20,000 fan letters a week. The Barbie fan club was created and immediately swelled to 8,500 chapters. Barbie became the best-selling girls toy ever. By the end of the 1960s, Barbie and her new friends were sold in 140 countries. Today, the typical girl between the ages of three and ten owns an average of eight Barbie dolls, and Mattel grosses more than $1 billion a year from Barbie-related sales.

Like many innovators, Ruth Handler knew that she was on to something special when she conceived of the seemingly oxymoronic adult doll for little girls. What she didn't know is that it would take so long to turn her conception into reality. And in that regard, she is in good company. It is the nature of innovation that an immediate brainstorm often takes years to come to fruition. When this is the case, the innovative company has an added burden. Aside from figuring out exactly how to manufacture the product, it must be equally sensitive to the possibility that its idea can be stolen.

Capitalism can be a ruthless game. Ted Turner once called rival Rupert Murdoch "a slimy character" and compared him to Adolph Hitler, to which Murdoch replied, quoting English prime minister Benjamin Disraeli, "Honorable sir, it's true that I am a low, mean snake. But you, sir, could walk beneath me wearing a top hat." But, while the two obviously never got along, there is no evidence that they spied on one another, which cannot be said for Oracle's Larry Ellison and Microsoft's Bill Gates.

During the Microsoft antitrust trial, Oracle's billionaire founder Larry Ellison hired Investigative Group International (IGI) to check up on some of Microsoft's Washington, D.C., connections. IGI reportedly offered janitors $1,200 to turn over Microsoft's garbage, literally. Ellison, while not denying the allegation, said that IGI used its own tactics, and he wasn't displeased. "They (Microsoft) are special," Ellison said. "They're the only ones in our industry that have been found guilty repeatedly of destroying companies. They destroyed Netscape; the most innovative company in Silicon Valley in a decade is gone."

So the innovative company is wise to keep its secrets secret while in production. So-called "stealth mode" is an established tactic that can and should be utilized when the task of bringing an innovation to market will take longer than desired. Harvard Business School professor Howard Stevenson states that stealth is a common business practice, noting that well-known real estate developers like Donald Trump often secretly buy tracts of land when they are trying to assemble parcels for projects. "If everyone knew who it was," says Stevenson, "the prices would go up."

Instant Image
The Split-Second Vision That Developed into the Polaroid Camera

Stealth was also the plan of action for Edwin Land and his Polaroid Corporation when developing instant picture technology. Back then, a time long before digital pictures, instant photography was not considered even remotely possible. Before the Polaroid Land camera, photography was an esoteric, expensive, protracted endeavor. But Edwin Land changed all that. To many, Land was considered a genius; a man who easily could have wound up in academia but chose to start a business for the freedom it allowed. Land was a man who had several inspirations over his life, inspirations that often took years to develop into a full-fledged product. And that was just fine with him.

"Over the years, I have learned that every significant invention has several characteristics," Land has observed. "By definition, it must be startling, unexpected, and must come to a world that is not prepared for it. If the world were prepared for it, it would not be much of an invention." He adds, "It is the public's role to resist. It is the duty of the inventor to build a new gestalt and to quietly substitute that gestalt for the old one in the framework of society. And when he does, his invention calmly and equitably becomes part of everyday life and no one can understand why it wasn't always there."

Land had his most startling, unexpected instant vision during World War II. At the time, Polaroid was not yet a name synonymous with photography. In fact, the company had never produced even a single photographic product, instead primarily producing products for the military in the war effort. One of Land's overriding concerns at the time was the peacetime endurance of his company. The solution, his great inspiration, the one that would provide him both an answer and an entirely new direction for his company, began far away from the laboratory where Land spent much of his time.

In the summer of 1943, Edwin Land and his wife Helen were vacationing in Santa Fe, New Mexico, with their three-year-old daughter Jennifer. Land stopped to snap a picture of the little girl. She posed and he clicked. Jennifer then asked to see the picture. Land said it was not ready. Confused, Jennifer asked how long it would be. Eureka!

Says Land, "Within an hour after the question, the camera, the film, and the physical chemistry became so clear that with a great sense of excitement I hurried to the place where a friend was staying, to describe to him in detail a camera that would give a picture immediately after exposure. In my mind it was so real that I spent several hours on this description." Land's previous work with polarizing lenses, plastics, and crystals coalesced in that moment, and Land later said that he "suddenly knew how to make a one-step photographic process."

Land envisioned a slim, pocket-sized camera that would allow the user to focus, shoot, and get a finished color picture in an instant. Given that photography was, at the time, a cumbersome, time-consuming, expensive process, it is no wonder why one biographer compared Edwin Land's inspiration to the Wright brothers visualizing a 200-passenger jetliner. Although Land understood in his head what he wanted to create, it would take another 29 years before the other necessary technologies would be available to allow him to fully implement his vision.

But that didn't stop Land from getting started. Within six months of that day in the desert, he had worked out most of the details of his new instant photography process. All R&D was done in stealth, even within his own company. Only Land and a few of his closest associates knew of the secret project. Although they were unable to come up with a camera that duplicated his initial vision, they were able to come up with a reasonable facsimile after about four years.

One hallmark of a great entrepreneur is that he knows his strengths and weaknesses. Edwin Land knew that his strengths were in physics and chemistry. Land could imagine the Polaroid camera and film but he needed someone to create the processes that would turn his camera idea into a mass-produced product. The engineering and mechanical phase of the project then fell upon Bill McCune. As one Polaroid employee put it, "Land told us what we were going to make. Bill McCune showed us how to make [it.]"

By 1947, the team had created a prototype and Land was able to demonstrate a crude instant picture camera to an amazed meeting of the Optical Society of America, held in the Hotel Pennsylvania in New York City. A year and a half later, the first instant camera was ready to hit the street. This first-ever Polaroid camera, the Model 95, weighed four pounds and sold for almost $100. For Polaroid, the camera was a dramatic shift in focus. Whereas the company had heretofore developed products for other businesses, it was, all of a sudden, in the business of mass-producing a consumer product, and all that entailed—marketing, publicity, sales, refunds, etc.

Again, Land was smart enough to know what he didn't know. He hired a vice president away from the Bell & Howell camera company to head Polaroid's new marketing division. That Polaroid had neither inventory nor a sales force was the least of J. Harold Booth's problems. At the time, in the postwar era, Polaroid had not yet transformed itself from a war company to a peacetime business, so money was in short supply. Booth had to sell a radically new product without an advertising budget. So Booth did what any good marketer would do, he turned his disadvantage into an advantage.

Booth came up with a marketing plan that would, hopefully, give the Polaroid Land Camera an aura of hard-to-get exclusivity and desirability while attracting some much-needed free publicity. In late 1948, Polaroid offered the camera for sale, but at only *one store* in the entire country—the Jordan Marsh department store in Boston. Newspapers picked up the story, described the unheard of phenomenon of instant pictures, and this unique, limited, new camera—the camera that no one could get—became the hottest ticket in town.

Booth then took the camera to Miami, figuring that vacationers would be more than willing to scoop up the hot new camera with the hefty price tag. He was right and the buzz buzzed. The Polaroid plan was to select one store in each of 30 cities and give that store an exclusive 30-day right to sell the camera. The idea was to create such a demand in selected cities around the country that there would be pent-up desire for the product when Polaroid could finally afford to roll the camera out nationally, and it worked.

In New York City, the nation's largest single market for photographic supplies, Macy's was selected to be the exclusive distributor of the Land camera. Not to be outdone, its archrival Gimbels scrambled, found an unnamed out-of-town supplier, and boldly announced that it too had the magic camera. Not to be outdone, Macy's sent a slew of clandestine employees armed with cash to Gimbels, and had them buy every Polaroid Land camera available. Gimbels was quickly out of stock and Macy's took out even larger ads in the *Times* and *Daily News* touting its *exclusive* sales of the cameras and film. In the first month of its exclusive contract, Macy's sold 4,000 cameras, a number that constituted one-half of Polaroid's total monthly production capabilities.

If you want to know how to market your new product, reread this section. Booth took a revolutionary new product and made it the must-have item of the day. That he did so out of necessity, without a budget, is all the more remarkable. As a result of his genius, owning a Polaroid instant camera became, for a while, like being the first person on the block to own a television set. In a very short time, Polaroid photography became part of the American landscape. Polaroid sold 500,000 Model 95s in the first five years and more than 200 million black and white images were snapped and instantly developed.

This is not to say, however, that there were not problems. For one, early Polaroid photographs had the nasty habit of fading over time; definitely not something you want your photos to do. Similarly, early efforts by Polaroid to create a color film were disheartening at best. What made Polaroid unique is that its CEO, Edwin Land himself, was intimately involved in designing the solutions for these and other vexing technical problems. (Land's positions at Polaroid included chairman of the board, CEO, *and* director of research.) Land was, first and foremost, an inventor and scientist. By the time he retired, he held some 500 patents.

And as an inventor, he never gave up his first vision— that of a small, graceful, affordable instant camera. By the late 1960s, Land felt that Polaroid was at a place where this dream could finally be realized. His instructions to his staff: Make the camera, and make it compact, integral, elegant, and garbage free (early Polaroid cameras created a mountain of trash as each picture had a layer that had to be peeled away and discarded). Says one engineer, "Land gave my boss a block of wood and told him that's how large the camera should be. He'd decided on that size by what would fit in his coat pocket. So, in essence, it was Land's tailor that determined the size of the camera." The camera of Land's dreams turned out to be the Polaroid SX-70.

Inside Polaroid, Land was revered, so that when he would, for instance, give a team a block of wood and tell them to make a camera out of it, they would. To Land, imagination was everything and he allowed his staff to concentrate on matters that interested them. He wanted a safe, humane workplace, and he stressed innovation over profits. Says Land, "The thing that drives the analysts wild is that we grow and grow and grow, not on the basis of the bottom line but on the basis of faith, that if you do your job well that the last thing you need to worry about is money; just as if you live right, you'll be happy." So Polaroid employees were equally committed to Land and believed in his vision. According to Polaroid vice president Sheldon Buckler, "There is no such thing as a simple invention. It has to be supported by a whole chain of equally difficult ideas. There were 100 places where most people would have said, 'There is no point in going on.'" The point is, they did go on.

The Polaroid SX-70 was the culmination of Land's quest to create the camera his daughter inspired. A cartridge of ten pictures was inserted into the back of the camera. Light entering the viewfinder hit four mirrors and was reflected onto the picture card. A motor grabbed the picture, passed it through the rollers and developing chemicals, and the card was ejected through a slot in the front. Elapsed time: one second. Years to create: almost 30.

The project was no easy feat. A device to shield the film had to be invented. A tiny, quiet, yet still powerful motor had to be created. To eliminate waste by-products, the film had to be designed to develop in sunlight with no protective layer to peel off, and so the SX-70 film contained 13 layers, which cost $100 million to develop and produce. In the end, Polaroid spent more than $600 million on an enterprise Land biographer Mark Olshaker says was "as complicated as the Manhattan Project [in order] to market and design a new amateur-oriented camera, all for the sake of a dream their idolized leader never gave up on." Was it worth it? Five years after the introduction of the SX-70, Polaroid's earnings topped $1 billion a year.

To Land and his staff, it was clearly worth it, and the money is not the reason. It sums up Land and his company when he says that his company "prospers most, and its members find their jobs most worthwhile, when its members are contributing their full talents and efforts to creating, producing, and selling products of outstanding merit."

It is probably not surprising that business innovation often requires bold leadership. Certainly that was the case with Edwin Land, who led his company by example. By all indications, it worked, and not just on the bottom line, but in those more ephemeral, yet equally important areas such as employee morale, commitment, and excitement. These qualities are all the more important when the business is committed to an innovative product, because, by its very nature, innovation requires people to be excited about something they can't see and don't understand. That is where the leader comes in. It is his or her job to keep the troops on their toes as they jointly venture forth into uncharted waters. If you think that's hard, just imagine the challenges that faced Joe Wilson, Tom McCullough, and Chester Carlson as they navigated the course for their tiny Haloid corporation for the 14 years it took to develop what *Fortune* called "the most successful product ever marketed in America."

The First Xerox Machine
The Slow Journey to Quick Copies

Chester Carlson was an only child whose parents died too young. As a result, he spent many hours alone tinkering, and had to work his way through junior college and then Cal Tech before receiving a degree in physics in 1930. Unable to get a job as a physicist, he eventually landed a position in the

New York City patent offices of a small electronics company, where his job was to assemble patent applications. Patent applications are extremely long documents and Carlson's job of duplicating the drawings and specifications was boring and tedious. Frustrated by his day job, and already prone to inventing, Carlson decided that there must be a better way.

He began to study photography, the physics of light, paper treatment, and printing. His months of research paid off when he stumbled upon photoconductivity—the method in which light affects the electrical conductivity of materials. Carlson figured that if he could use light to cast an image—a sort of shadow—he could then use photoconductivity to capture that image and transfer it onto paper, thereby cre-ating a more efficient copying process. While working at his patent job during the day, and attending law school by night, Carlson somehow found time in the ensuing three years to perfect what he called "electronphotograhy." Final-ly, on October 22, 1938 (10-22-38), in the Astoria apartment building that housed his crude laboratory, Carlson created a blurry but legible electronphotographic copy that read "10-22-38 Astoria." 47 years later, in 1985, that piece of pa-per would become part of the permanent collection of the Smithsonian.

But back in 1938, at the height of the Great Depression, Chester Carlson was hardly seen as a visionary, and barely had enough money to live on, let alone market his product. Nevertheless, in 1939, he was able to scrape together a few hundred dollars (a princely sum at the time) to have a proto-type made. It didn't work. Another was made, and it worked only briefly. Soon the war diverted everyone's attention, and Carlson went back to demonstrating his process by hand, us-ing manual plates.

Hoping to find a corporate sponsor for his invention, or anyone who would buy it Carlson then spent the next few years meeting with, and getting turned down by, the likes of GE, RCA, and IBM. Why would anyone need this machine when carbon paper worked just fine? His years of fruitless leads brought him financial ruin and, eventually, divorce. Carlson then persuaded a small, private foundation—the Battelle Memorial Institute—to continue research on his invention, signing a royalty-sharing agreement with the Columbus, Ohio, firm in 1944.

The break he had been hoping for came in 1947. It was then that Joe Wilson, the president of a small photographic company called Haloid, and his chief engineer, John Dessaur, traveled from Rochester, New York, to Ohio to see for themselves the electronphotograhy machine they had read about some time earlier in the journal *Radio-Electronic Engineering*. As a boy in Rochester, Wilson had grown up near Kodak's largest manufacturing plant, Kodak Park. While other boys dreamed of being Babe Ruth or Joe DiMaggio, Joe Wilson grew up dreaming of creating a business like George Eastman's Kodak—a business that changed lives and impacted the world.

But in 1947, Haloid, the company founded by Wilson's father, was not that company; it was only a small photographic manufacturing operation. Yet Joe Wilson was nothing if not a visionary. In later years, Wilson would talk about how great their company could be. Says associate Sol Linowitz, "When Joe would make some of his prophecies, people would wonder what he was smoking. Joe was always someone who saw things with great optimism." When Joe Wilson died in 1971, they found on him a small, blue index card that he apparently always carried. It summarized his life's goals: "To be a whole man; to attain serenity through the creation of a family life of uncommon richness; through leadership of a business which brings happiness to its workers, serves its customers, and brings prosperity to its owners; by aiding a society threatened by fratricidal division to gain unity."

So in 1947, when Wilson and Dessaur headed to Columbus, they hoped to find that product—that magic product—that could fulfill Wilson's big dreams. After watching a demonstration of Carlson's electronphotograhy process, Wilson exclaimed, "Of course, it's got a million miles to go before it will be marketable. But when it does become marketable, we've got to be in the picture!" They signed an agreement that called for Haloid to develop and fund Carlson's machine.

In one of their first steps, team Haloid decided that they needed to rename the process. Several names were bandied about, but "Kleen Kopy," "Magic Printer," and "Dry Duplicator" just didn't have the ring that Joe Wilson was looking for. Finally, a language professor was hired. He suggested they combine the Greek words *xeros* (dry) and *graphein* (to write) and thus call the process xerography. Many years later, after the company's entire operations and the first few million dollars had been committed to the development of xerography, Haloid needed a name change as well, to represent the technology it was banking on. Neither American Xerography Corporation or National Xerographic, Inc. felt quite right. Then one morning, Wilson was walking near his home with his associate Sol Linowitz when they happened upon a sign that read "Kodak." Both men knew the famous story of how George Eastman had coined the name because he liked the sound *k* made and wanted it at both ends of his company's name. "Doesn't that make sense?" Linowitz asked. "Xerox, with an *x* at the end," he added. Haloid became Haloid Xerox, and soon, just Xerox. Joe Wilson's dream of being like George Eastman was coming true in more ways than one.

But back in 1948, initial progress on the machine was exceedingly slow. An early brochure described the 39 steps it took to make a copy on the first-ever commercial copier, the Model A Xerox, which was often referred to as the "Ox

Box" because of its huge size and slow speed. The Model A took three minutes to make a single print and an operator had to be on hand to transfer each individual copy from one part of the machine to another. Test sites confirmed what Haloid already knew—a machine that was too complex was a machine that was unwanted.

Still, Wilson and Carlson forged ahead. Interestingly, Carlson was never on the Xerox payroll, though he was often invited to join the company. He preferred the independence being a consultant afforded him. He was also exceptionally protective of his invention, even amongst Haloid employees. Carlson would go so far as to mix the coatings for the toner in his private basement at home and then bring them to the Haloid labs. Even today, these formulas are one of Xerox's best kept secrets. They have never been patented to keep the exact contents unknown.

Wilson though was not a private man; he was the extroverted visionary in this dynamic duo. He was the one who kept the ship afloat in a vigilant effort to see their dream and commitment through. Fourteen years is a very long time to keep an organization, any organization, committed to a common goal. It was even difficult for Haloid (as it was still known at the time) because the goal was totally unrelated to its core business. Not only did Wilson have to keep Haloid's 50-year-old photographic supply business going, he had to get the company ready for the change that he saw coming. To succeed, he had to have an unwavering commitment to his business acumen and he had to convey this commitment to Haloid's employees, investors, officers, and board members. As one Haloid veteran puts it, "Xerography went through many stages in its development at which any sane management committee would have been justified in turning it down." Part of this steadfastness was Wilson's frayed blue index card, and part of this was economic reality. Says Horace Becker, an early Xerox employee who helped create the first working Xerox machine, the 914, "The reason the 914 became such a success at the Haloid Company was that if [Carlson] had gone anywhere else, and that company had anything else to do, they would have lost interest in it. Joe Wilson was facing a shrinking marketplace with his products and it was xerography or nothing."

The 914 (so named because it could reproduce documents up to 9 inches by 14 inches in size) cost $75 million to develop, which may seem like a small sum in today's world, but was more than Haloid's total earnings from 1950 through 1959. All told, it took the company 14 years to develop the first workable photocopy machine, which debuted 21 years after Chester Carlson made his famous "10-22-38 Astoria" image. Says Linowitz, "None of us really saw how big it would be." (This was true in a literal sense as well: The 914 was a behemoth, standing three and a half feet high, four feet long, four feet wide, and weighing 648 pounds. "It was a God-awful big desk," laments ex-president Becker.)

Xerox was not alone in underestimating the 914. In 1959, when Haloid announced the introduction of the world's first mass market commercial copier, the business press yawned. The *New York Times* completely ignored the announcement, the *Wall Street Journal* gave it a scant five-paragraph, buried story, *Financial World* had a seven-paragraph story, and *Forbes* decided not to run a story at all because Haloid had "only $19 million in assets." Only *Business Week* saw the 914 for the revolutionary product it really was, putting Joe Wilson and the 914 on its September 1959 cover.

The 914 was not the only copier on the block at the time. There were actually about 35 different companies making copiers, using five different methods, all of which were too slow to make an impact on the workplace. Some created translucent originals that had to be peeled apart by hand, while others had to be soaked in an activating solution, making the process too long and cumbersome to be of much use. What they did have going for them was that they were cheap, reflecting their quality. Priced in the $300 to $400 range, these machines were in use because they were relatively inexpensive.

The 914 on the other hand was a marvel of simplicity. The operator merely had to place the original face down on a glass tray, dial the desired number of copies (up to 15), push a button, and presto—out popped clean, easy-to-read copies. But with this simplicity, and the corresponding millions of dollars it took to make the machine so simple, the cost of a Xerox copier needed to be priced at $40,000; far too high for almost all businesses, and Xerox was well aware of this.

This is the part of the story where Joe Wilson's genius may have matched Chester Carlson's. Says Becker, "Joe Wilson and company came up with the absolutely fantastic invention that was more important than xerography, the decision to rent the machines. We rented the 914 for $95 a month, for which you got 2,000 free copies, and four cents for each additional copy." Like the movie theatre that makes its real money selling popcorn, not movie tickets, Xerox decided to make its money selling copies, not copiers. The leasing plan allowed customers to try out the 914 without making a huge capital investment. Because the copies were so easy to make, clean, easy to read, and above all, extremely useful, the copying revolution was born. (In 1985, a Burke Marketing research study proved how easy and convenient copying had become by concluding that 29 percent of all copies were unnecessary; in all, 130 billion wasted copies a year). By 1967, there were 9,000 914s being leased around the world, and each one brought in $4,500 in revenue. Each copier averaged about 100,000 copies a year, far in excess of the 24,000 copy allowance.

Needless to say, the Xerox 914 quickly became a cash cow. In 1962, two years after the introduction of the 914,

Xerox cracked the *Fortune 500* for the first time, coming in at 423. By 1965, Xerox had 7,000 employees. Says Eric Steenburgh, a manager at the time, "I personally hired 50 to 100 people a month during the boom." Company revenues exploded, cracking the $1 billion per year mark in 1968, with $134 million in profits (and this, a mere nine years after *Forbes* concluded that Haloid's $19 million in assets were too puny to notice). By 1970, Xerox was 40 on the *Fortune 500* list. Today, Xerox has become one of those rare household words that can be either a noun or a verb ("Would you please xerox this for me?"), and the company has more than 100,000 employees. Joe Wilson's dream of building a company like Kodak is one that can be safely checked off his to-do list.

By their very nature, innovators are a unique breed. Often headstrong, unusually creative, always committed, and unwaveringly self-confident, innovators who bring great ideas to market are just a tad different than the rest of us. But maybe that's what it takes to commit so fully to a vision that you are willing to take the big risk necessary to see your dream come to fruition. When it works, the great business innovation is a classic win-win: The invention is a boon to society and the entrepreneur reaps the financial rewards of a job well done. We are fortunate indeed that there are such men and women among us.

Freedom Fighter
Liberating People from Wheelchairs
with the iBot

Multimillionaire entrepreneur and inventor Dean Kamen has been called the Thomas Edison of medicine. But really, that description doesn't do him justice. Yes he is a genius, medical and otherwise, but what sets Kamen apart from most other inventors, and most other entrepreneurs for that matter, is not that he invents things that he thinks will make money, but that he invents things that he thinks *ought* to exist, regardless of market demand. "I don't work on a project unless I believe that it will dramatically improve life for a bunch of people," says Kamen.

While Kamen was attending college in the 1970s, his brother—then a medical student—complained that there was no reliable way to give steady doses of drugs to patients. So Kamen invented the first portable infusion pump capable of delivering drugs to patients who had previously required around-the-clock monitoring, freeing them from a life inside the hospital.

Freeing people is something that he likes to do and something he does very well. Prior to Kamen, kidney dialysis machines were monstrously large contraptions—the size of a washing machine, and patients needing dialysis were required to make regular trips to dialysis centers. Baxter International, a medical development company, thought that a smaller dialysis machine was possible and contracted with Kamen's privately held company, DEKA Research & Development (DEKA), to develop an alternative to the cumbersome machines. But even Baxter was amazed when DEKA came back a few years later with a dialysis machine that was not only smaller, but portable—no bigger than a phone book. Says Vernon Loucks, former chair of Baxter

International, "We didn't believe it could be done. Now it's all over the world. Dean is the brightest guy I've ever met in this business, bar none."

So it might be said that Dean Kamen is in the freedom business, and it is no wonder, for a free soul he is. Kamen is a self-taught, college-dropout physicist who lives in a hexagonally shaped house of his own design atop a hill just outside Manchester, New Hampshire. His estate, called Westwind, is powered by a wind turbine, has a pulley system that delivers a bottle of wine from the kitchen to the bedroom, is outfitted with a softball field, and is full of toys, including a jukebox, a slot machine, and a 25-ton steam engine once owned by Henry Ford. In Westwind's basement, there is a foundry, a machine shop, and a computer room. His wood-paneled library is full of awards and honorary degrees: In 2000, Kamen was awarded the National Medal of Technology by President Clinton for "inventions that have advanced medical care worldwide, and for innovative and imaginative leadership in awakening America to the excitement of science and technology."

Kamen houses a 1913 Model T Ford, a Porsche 928, and a black Humvee in one garage, and two helicopters in the other. The smaller, piston-driven copter takes him to and from work at his offices in downtown Manchester as he listens to the theme from *Star Wars* on a headset. The larger, turbine-driven chopper is reserved for longer trips, such as to his private island off the coast of Connecticut. For trips more than a few hundred miles, he flies his twin-turbofan Citation jet. But none of these is his coolest mode of transportation.

That honor goes to the Independence 3000 iBot Transporter, Kamen's true nod toward freedom. For starters, this "wheelchair" can climb stairs, cross curbs, and traverse sand. The iBot can roll smoothly on two, four, or six wheels, and in the two-wheel position, the user can be raised to the same eye-level he or she would be in when standing. This alone makes the iBot a wonder. A person confined to a wheelchair spends his or her life looking up at people. Imagine sitting in a supermarket, hitting the iBot's "stand" button and swiveling up onto two wheels to reach something on the top shelf. What must it be like for people who have lost their legs to again face the world standing up?

Maybe the most technologically amazing thing about the iBot is its ability to negotiate almost any path, including grass, sand, rocks, carpeting, steep stairs, and high curbs, without tipping. It does so by using a battery of onboard sensors and gyroscopes that allow it to automatically readjust itself to changes in the terrain and its user's center of gravity. When confronted with an activity that requires a change in its current settings, the iBot polls its three internal computers and various sensors, which "vote" on the correct action to take depending on the data it has gathered and its user's commands.

Yet, while the end result is a marvel, the path getting there was anything but. Kamen says that he had no idea how difficult it would be, and how long it would actually take, to create his product when he conceived of it almost a decade earlier. At the time, Kamen witnessed a young man struggling to get his wheelchair up a curb. "I just fixated on how unreasonable that condition really is," he says. "And it just seemed to me that the fundamental issue was the world has not been architected for people that are sitting down at 39 inches." So Dean Kamen decided then and there to create a better wheelchair. And unlike some large companies, he gave no thought to what it would cost to do so, or who would eventually buy it. Instead, he committed himself, his considerable resources, and his company, to solving a problem he thought ought to be solved.

Kamen began by thinking about this old problem in a new way. Instead of creating a chair that could go upstairs, what if he could make a machine that could stand up and balance the way humans do? "Your mother remembers your first steps. It's a big deal that humans walk erect," says Kamen. "It's difficult to do. But once we've learned to do it, we're capable of dealing with curbs and a world with stairs." But this was easier said than done.

The first wheelchair was made in 1650 by a man named Johann Haustach of Nuremberg for the legless Stephan Farfler who propelled it with hand cranks. In 1932, engineer Harry Jennings built the first folding, tubular steel wheelchair for a paraplegic friend named Herbert Everest. Together they founded Everest & Jennings, a company that so monopolized the wheelchair market that an antitrust suit was brought against it by the Department of Justice, charging the company with fixing wheelchair prices.

Kamen was not the first man either to conceive of a stair-climbing wheelchair; in fact, the problems faced by those before him only show how intractable this problem had been. "The problems of climbing stairs in a device other than a tank are formidable," says Stanley Sobel, a nationally known rehabilitation engineer. "Stairs are not all of standard length, height, or width. In addition, an individual's mass and how that is positioned, is a major variable." Patents on designs from the 1950s and 1970s led nowhere. By the early 1990s, advances in electronic controls made designs for all-terrain wheelchairs much more feasible, and Quest Technologies actually designed and built a wheelchair that successfully climbed stairs. The huge chair would wheel on flat surfaces then deploy a set of tracks when climbing stairs (as long as they were not too steep). It required four batteries, each weighing about 50 pounds. "It had the look and feel of a tank," Sobel says.

So the challenge before Kamen was formidable. The breakthrough came when Kamen slipped in the shower, then caught himself by swinging his arms. He figured that if he could do it, a computer should easily be able to replicate the process of rebalancing a mechanical object like a wheelchair. "Walking is really a controlled fall," Kamen realized. To create such a machine, however, would require substantial technical and computer integration. Kamen and his engineers came up with a two-wheeled balancing prototype that worked and became a top-secret patented invention crammed full of sophisticated gyroscopes, electric motors, and computers. Kamen also realized that it would take money—plenty of money—and much more time, to mass-produce this item and bring his inspiration to full fruition. So he decided to seek out a partner. Kamen targeted Johnson & Johnson, even though the company never made a wheelchair before. But this unique opportunity was difficult to pass up and they struck a deal. After another six years and $100 million in design and testing, the iBot was born.

"Dean and his group solved the problem of balance," said Dr. Robert Gussin, Johnson & Johnson's retired vice president of technology. "The iBot uses gyros, sensors, and very sophisticated software to keep the center of gravity underneath the seat. It can balance. It does not need a bigger and bigger base to remain stable." That has always been the problem in the past. "This is like when you were a kid and you balanced a broomstick in your hand," Gussin adds. "It starts to sway and you move under it. This essentially does the same thing, only it does it very, very quickly."

To Kamen, the wheelchair is "the world's most sophisticated robot." After all, the sleek 200-pound vehicle (smaller than a conventional motor-powered wheelchair) is powered by four transmissions, six gyroscopes, and three computer systems—making it more akin to the helicopters Kamen once designed than to a traditional wheelchair. To prove what his invention could do, Kamen once hopped in his iBot and climbed the stairs from a Paris Métro station to the restaurant level of the Eiffel Tower. Needless to say, the iBot isn't cheap. At a cost of $20,000 to $25,000 per chair, it is at least twice as expensive as the average motorized wheelchair. But by the same token, the iBot can save users money by making it easier to stay on a job or, more importantly, obviate the need to retrofit a home with wider doorways, ramps, and mechanical lifts, all of which can easily cost $35,000.

But even more than money, "what will influence people most is the ability to be at eye level and reach things," Gussin says. "A lot of the wheelchair users who have used the iBot report that it is like being able to stand up again. There's even that slight sway that you experience, that feeling of balance. It is a powerful experience for someone who has been below eye level in a wheelchair for a long time." According to Woodie Flowers, a mechanical engineering professor at MIT and a friend of Kamen's, that's just what the freedom fighter was hoping for. "He's not one to get caught up in conventional wisdom."

The Innovation Rules

- When it will take longer than desired to get an innovation to market, it is incumbent upon the innovator to keep the plans secret; operate in stealth mode.

- Teams are often more successful than a lone wolf, especially when patience is required.

- Innovation that makes life better almost always will find a market.

!!!!!!!!!!!!!!!!!!!!!!!!!

The Seven
Great Lessons
of Innovation

Innovation is one of the most sought after, talked about attributes in business. Seminars are held about it, CEOs stress it, managers are supposed to reward it, yet all to often, innovation is more theory than practice. Because problems can arise anywhere—whether convincing the suits that the idea merits further discussion or marketing to consumers that don't even know that they need the item—initiating and implementing an innovative idea is rarely easy. It often takes a genius idea, several failures, total commitment, and plenty of money before the breakthrough product is seen by the public for what it is—something truly unique and extraordinary that can make their lives better in some way.

But innovation *is* possible. It need not be another corporate goal. It can instead be a real road that the business innovator can travel on to reach his destination. But just how do you get there? You need a map, of course. A pilot intent on flying from Los Angeles to New York doesn't just take off from LAX and hope to get to La Guardia. Instead, he creates a flight plan that explains exactly how he will get to his destination. That is what the innovator must do. You have to have an end place in mind and create a plan for getting there. The problem is that a map to business innovation success has not been available. Until now.

It is said that success leaves clues. If you want to know how to innovate, you don't have to reinvent the wheel. A far better method is to see how other business innovators accomplished their goals and learn from them. You do not have to make the same mistakes they made. Mistakes are here to teach us lessons, so it would behoove the innovator to learn those lessons. Understanding the lessons, all seven of them, from the introduction of previous products will enable you to create your own map and lead you safely down the road to entrepreneurial success.

1. Think of Things That Never Were and Ask, "Why Not?"

Bobby Kennedy's famous motto, adapted from George Bernard Shaw, is an apt description of the first ingredient necessary to create a great new product. Terrific products come from inspired ideas, and inspiration can strike at any time. When George de Mestral took that annoying burr from his sock and placed it underneath his microscope, creating a breakthrough product like Velcro was the last thing on his mind. But what he saw changed his life. De Mestral spent the next ten years trying to duplicate artificially what nature made effortlessly. His inspiration was so profound that he was willing to make whatever sacrifices were necessary to see his idea through to completion.

Most breakthrough products follow a similar arc, although some time lines are shorter. Once inspired, it is incumbent upon the innovator, if he or she is truly committed to making a difference, to see the product through. Ruth Handler had long envisioned an adult doll for girls to play with, but was unable to get anyone else at Mattel interested in her idea until she saw a similar doll in a store window in France. But even then it took several years to create Barbie. Yet she never gave up on her initial inspiration. This kind of zealotry is essential if a new product is ever to become a household name. The innovator must be so inspired by an idea, with a clear intent, that the consciousness of consumers cannot help but be swayed by his or her will. Without someone devoted to an intense revelation, the innovative product is doomed to mediocrity.

The would-be innovator need not wait for the idea to strike him out of the blue. Earl Tupper spent much of his life actively looking to make a difference; to invent something useful, original, radical. His advice? "To invent useful and successful inventions, those with inventive minds should not be afraid to look far, far into the future and visualize the things that might be. Remember, the things which are so commonplace today would have been the ravings of a fanatic a few years ago." Tupperware wasn't even invented until Tupper was in his 40s, and even then, not until other Tupper products failed to make a dent.

As Shaw says, "Some men look at things that are and ask 'Why?' I think of things that never were and ask 'Why not?'" If you think of such things, sooner or later, that million-dollar idea may come.

2. The Power of One

The second lesson in innovation is that one person can make a difference. Whatever product you look at, you will invariably find that there was some man or woman behind it who was steadfastly committed to its success. It is this combination of sheer audacity and bold tenacity that can make the difference between unbridled success and desolate failure. If a product is to become a star, someone must champion it. That's the bottom line. His or her commitment must be so total that the obstacles ahead, and obstacles *are* ahead, will fuel the fire rather than dampen his or her resolve.

Remember Al Neuharth? When the self-proclaimed S.O.B. decided to take $1 million out of Gannett's discretionary budget to analyze whether there was a market for *USA Today,* he showed his resolve, and when he allocated almost a half a billion dollars to actually get the thing off the ground, he proved how totally committed he was. Either way, *USA Today* would never have been born had Neuharth not been its champion. Whether you are talking about Velcro or the Palm Pilot or Silly Putty, what you see is someone who had an idea that was impossible to let go.

For most entrepreneurs, that should not be a problem. Entrepreneurs are, by and large, a fairly obsessed lot. They are also ego-driven. And that is good because it takes a self-directed, dedicated individual to take an untested, unproven idea, hitch his wagon to it, and ride it to the stars, or bankruptcy court. Indeed, there are no guarantees that the idea that you think is so great is a notion that will be shared by millions of other people. But unless you believe in your idea, unless you think that you have the greatest thing since sliced bread, don't even think about venturing down this path. Because it will take all of your best skills, ideas, and efforts to make a go of it.

The entrepreneur behind a new product can be a one-man show or part of a larger organization. Either way, the product still needs the backing of a visionary individual. While it may be true that the path to product placement and a sultan's riches is easier if the individual is part of a corporation or some other large organization, it's not necessarily so. When Commander Eugene McDonald decided to create a wireless remote control for television sets, he was fortunate indeed that his Zenith Corporation had the resources, both in terms of money and people, to implement his ideas. And when McDonald tapped Robert Alder to create the remote, Adler was able to do so because he had the money of Zenith behind him. But without these two visionaries, you would likely still be getting up to change channels.

By the same token, while the resources of a group can help the individual, it is not a requirement of the job. Douglas Englebart worked at one of the most prestigious research facilities in the world when he was creating the computer mouse, but his higher-ups at the Stanford Research Institute didn't quite understand what he was doing. So although he certainly had access to some of the best minds around, Englebart was more akin to the lone wolf innovator who has to battle the business elements to get his product out there. The best of all possible worlds would be the one where the visionary individual has the solid backing of his organization, thereby giving him the means necessary to implement his vision without risking massive personal failure.

Probably far more common is the situation where an individual, on his own, gets an idea and decides to risk it all in pursuit of a dream. Ed Lowe was nothing but a young, ambitious veteran with tons of unsold clay when he decided that he had a better cat litter. Crisscrossing the country in his old car, bartering his way into cat shows, and changing cat boxes one at a time is what it took for him to make Kitty Litter a success. Chris Haney and Scott Abbot really thought they had something unique with Trivial Pursuit, and bet the bank that others would agree.

The good news here twofold. First, inspiration can strike at anytime, and the struck individual can turn that idea into a success whether he is part of a group or working on his own. The principle in either case is the same: Someone must believe in the product, no holds barred. When a driven individual has a cool new product, the opportunity for entrepreneurial success exists.

Second, and just as important, the experience of all of these business innovators proves that one need not be a brilliant inventor or scientist to succeed, because the product dominance dance is a two-step. Yes, the first step is the creation of an innovative product. But just as important is the marketing of that product. When scientists at GE created a synthetic rubber alternative they named gupp, no one knew what to do with it. A use was not found until Peter Hodgson saw it at a cocktail party and thought that it might make a great toy. Silly Putty was the creation of a great marketer who knew something unique when he saw it.

So the configuration can take many forms: The crucial individual could be a brilliant scientist who works in a large corporation (Chester Carlson at Xerox) or a solo marketing genius (Bette Nesmith and Liquid Paper). An innovator could be the solo scientist (Buckminster Fuller and the geodisic dome) or the marketer who is part of a team (J. Mays and Freeman Thomas at Volkswagen). It really doesn't matter. What matters is that the person wanting to create the next big thing be committed and dynamic in pursuit of the dream.

3. Keep It Simple, Stupid

No, no one is calling you dumb. Rather, the rule—keep it simple, stupid, and its acronym KISS—is a great way to remember the third lesson of innovation. When you create something new and offer it for sale, you are also asking people to give up something tried and true. While change gets a lot of lip service, people over 30 don't really change all that easily or readily. So, if you are going to offer them something new and improved, make sure that it is simple and does one or two things *very well*. The last thing people need is some sort of Rube Goldberg contraption. People buy VCRs, not because they hope to program the machine to tape something next Wednesday evening at 10:00, but because they can hit "record" and leave the room.

The more complicated something is, the less likely it is to be a breakout product. This was a lesson Jeff Hawkins had to learn the hard way. Hawkins's first attempt at a personal digital assistant (PDA), the Zoomer, tried to be all things to all nerds. It was only when Hawkins realized that people didn't want a replacement for their computer, but a simple device that kept addresses and appointments, that the Palm Pilot was born.

The simpler the product is, and the more that it solves one problem very, very well, the greater the likelihood that it will become an indispensable tool. Gertrude Tenderich and Ellery Mann took over the Tampax Corporation because they knew that they had a unique product that solved one problem well. The same is true of Victor Mills and his team at Procter & Gamble when they began to create the first disposable diaper. The prototype versions, with pins and plastic, didn't fit quite right or work all that well. It was only when they improved it and made the product super simple that mothers were willing to put the product on their beloved children. Because disposables were better than what the moms were using, and because they were simple and made life easier, the product soon became a fact of life.

Keeping it simple is even more important when you want to create a machine or some electronics product. It is easy to get baffled by a new product with pages of instructions. The simpler the core function can be kept, the better. The reason that the Xerox 914 became the biggest thing in business machines was that it made copying simple. Turn the knob to the desired number of copies and push "print." That was all there was to it. While there were other machines on the market at the time, none came close to the market dominance of the 914 because none was as easy to use as the 914. The reasons the Lisa computer failed were that it was slow and expensive because its user interface was so new. The Polaroid SX-70 on the other hand allowed you to take a picture and see the finished photograph in about a minute. No focusing required, no trips to the drug store necessary.

Complicated products, on the other hand, have almost no chance of becoming something special because people generally do not want to take the time necessary to learn how to use them. Think about all of those PDAs at your local office supply store. One reason they are not as successful as the Palm Pilot is because many of them are far too complicated to be understood in a short amount of time. On the other hand, the microwave oven has remained deceptively simple for years.

The lesson is clear: KISS and grow rich.

4. First Is Best

Getting your product to market first can often mean the difference between having a winner and being a loser. This is not always true, but it is true enough that it can be stated as rule number 4. The so-called first mover's advantage goes to the company that is first to establish its product in a given market. Post-its were first. Kitty Litter was first. Tupperware was first. Pampers were first. Barbie was first. Even a lead as little as a few months can create an insurmountable market position. Yahoo! and Ebay remain where they are today, despite the entry of many other similar companies, because they were the first significant players in their field.

There are three main reasons why the first mover's advantage is especially critical when it comes to new product innovation. The first has to do with distribution. By being first to market, a company is forced to open up a distribution channel, which itself is no easy feat. Getting your product to a place where people can see it and buy it is critical to its success. In fact, a main reason Palm agreed to the U.S. Robotics buyout was that Palm did not have a large distribution channel and U.S. Robotics did. By being first, you blaze a distribution path that your competitors may not be able to duplicate. The market dominance afforded *USA Today* is due in no small measure to its having a distribution channel that its competitors could not replicate. Not only do competitors lag behind you chronologically, but by being first with a hot product, you may have enough clout to block their full-fledged entry into the market. Moreover, your distribution partners may be reluctant to sell competing goods so as to not offend you or lose your business.

The second advantage of the being first is that you are painting on a clean canvas and thereby have a unique chance to create a great name for yourself. First impressions count, and by being first, you have an opportunity to make sure that the public's first impression of you and your product is a favorable one. Because it is almost assured that the first impression is the one that will last, being first is a golden opportunity. For example, by being the first toothpaste in history to offer fluoride, along with the stamped approval of the American Dental Association, Crest burned itself forever in America's psyche. By the same token, when the De-Lorean was introduced to poor reviews, and then when its namesake founder was caught on video allegedly dealing cocaine, the ill will created was almost impossible to reverse.

Finally, the first mover's advantage gives you an edge-up in terms of experience. When Marc Grégoire learned how to attach Teflon to aluminum, a feat no one else had been able to accomplish, thereby creating Teflon-coated cookware, he gained an experiential advantage evident to this day. While many of the knock-off Teflon pans that followed his to the market were shabby and poorly made, Grégoire's trial-and-error experience enabled him to offer a superior Teflon pan. Even today, French-made Tefal pans are considered the best.

5. Try, Try Again

The path of the innovator may not follow a straight line, grasshopper. Getting a product right often takes trial and error, followed by a few mistakes, a couple of bonehead moves, and only then, maybe, a home run. When Dr. Percy Spencer noticed that the chocolate bar in his pocket melted after standing near a magnetron tube, he realized that something unique had occurred. Yet the first microwave oven took years to develop, and even then was 5½ feet tall, weighed over 750 pounds, and cost more than $5,000. It would take years of trial and error before Raytheon was able to create a "radar range" that could be used by the public.

The same was true in the development of the Gillette Mach 3 razor. Scientists at Gillette spent years trying to figure out how to make a triple-bladed razor. It took more than 500 engineers, with degrees from places like M.I.T. and Stanford, to build the razor, and even then, it was accomplished only after Gillette spent more than $750 million and ten years in development. All told, Gillette received 35 patents for a razor that is dipped in carbon and bonded with niobium, a rare tin alloy normally used in superconducting magnets. More than anything else, the lesson from Gillette is that the business that wants to innovate must be willing to stay in it for the long haul and allocate the resources, both human and capital, necessary to see the project through to completion.

Of course, most companies don't have the assets of Gillette, and that's okay. Bette Nesmith certainly didn't when she came up with Liquid Paper (coincidentally later bought out by Gillette for $47.5 million). Ms. Nesmith tinkered with her product on her kitchen table, trying different permutaions in her effort to create a thick, quick-drying correction fluid. But she stuck with it, learned her lessons, endured the tough times, and succeeded as a result. While some products are right from the start—Kitty Litter, for example—more often, the innovator must be willing to create beta versions and iron out the kinks before the product is accepted by the fickle marketplace. But if you put in the effort, and you have the right product, a little corner of the world can be yours.

6. Risky Business

If an entrepreneur is a person who takes a risk with money to make money, then a business innovator must make one *uber*-entrepreneur. Starting a business is tough enough, but starting a business around a radically new product is almost masochistic. It will not be an easy path. Will it be exciting, crazy, fun, exasperating, rewarding, frightening, and challenging? You bet. But it won't be easy.

Creating an innovative product and getting it out there often takes everything an entrepreneur has to offer. The financial risks involved, not to mention the emotional toll, are considerable indeed. When two auto designers in California created a new car using a secret budget and dared their German superiors to take a risk on a car their bosses associated with Hitler, they were risking their careers. And when VW agreed to produce the new Beetle, it risked being perceived as a backward-looking company. Innovation requires risk, it is as simple as that.

The risk is probably even more acute when the entrepreneurs do not have a large corporation and a steady paycheck to fall back on. Chris and John Haney, Scott Abbot, and Ed Werner risked personal bankruptcy when they bet the ranch on Trivial Pursuit. It was only when they found a bank willing to give them a line of credit that the men were able to turn their dream into reality. This sort of high-wire act may be necessary to score big. Not only did Babe Ruth hold the record for most home runs in history for over 50 years, but he also held the record for the most strikeouts. Swinging for the fences means risking a strikeout.

7. Synergy Is Necessary

Synergy, a word coined by geodesic dome inventor Buckminster Fuller, is, according to Fuller "the behavior of wholes unpredicted by the behavior of its parts." The concept is generally thought to be that the whole is greater than the sum of its parts, but that is only partially correct. It is more accurate to think that when people join in a united effort, what they can accomplish together cannot always be predicted by who they are individually. For a product to succeed wildly, synergy is usually necessary.

Take the Palm Pilot, for instance. Although Jeff Hawkins is undoubtedly a brilliant engineer, he needed someone who could steer his genius toward business success. That person was Donna Dubinsky. Together, these two made a formidable team. The Palm Pilot, a result of their synergistic efforts, came about because what they could do together was so much more than what each could have done alone. Dubinsky needed Hawkins's mind, and Hawkins needed Dubinsky's business acumen. It was their yin and yang, forming a better whole, which allowed them to make the Palm Pilot what it is.

The same can be said for Earl Tupper and Brownie Wise. While Tupper had the ingenuity to create a new plastic and a new container, it was Wise who was able to figure out a way to get America to buy the product. Without her, we never would have heard of him, and vice versa. Chester Carlson was able to duplicate "10-22-38 Astoria" on a machine, but was unable on his own to interest anyone in his invention, including GE, RCA, and IBM. Joe Wilson wanted to turn his tiny Haloid photographic company into a world powerhouse, but had no way to do so. It was only when Wilson, and his soon-to-be-renamed Xerox Corporation, and Chester Carlson joined forces that both were able to accomplish their individual dreams. Steve Jobs needed Steve Wozniack to make Apple Computer. Gertrude Tenderich needed Ellery Mann to turn Tampax into a household word. And Spencer Silver needed Art Fry to make Post-its a reality. That is synergy.

The would-be business innovator should bear this lesson in mind. Generally speaking, entrepreneurs who want to turn the world on its head with the next great thing are egomaniacs, in the best sense of the word. That is, they so believe in themselves, and in their cause and abilities, that they think they can do it all on their own. And often they can. Richard Branson created Virgin largely based on his own vision and drive. Jeff Bezos created Amazon.com. Mrs. Debbie Fields invented the modern cookie store. Yet even these visionaries had help—lots of help.

It is necessary for the innovator to understand what his or her strengths and weaknesses are and then look for teammates who can fill the gaps. Something truly extraordinary can happen, does happen, when the right people get together behind the inspired vision. The exciting thing is that what happens is, in fact, unpredictable. But not knowing is part of the fun. That is why we play the game. There is simply no telling how far the right people and the right product can go.

Whatever You Can Do, Begin It

Great innovation stems from bold action. Buckminster Fuller tried to kill himself before realizing that the answers he sought could not be learned from anyone but himself. Douglas Engelbart decided that a life of risk beat one of quiet desperation, and that decision begat the computer mouse. Dean Kamen decided to build a better wheelchair because he saw a man in a conventional wheelchair struggling over a curb one day. Peter Hodgson was $12,000 in debt and still borrowed another $147 to buy and sell Silly Putty.

No one will give you permission to be bold, but boldness is a requirement for this job. As M.H. Lawrence wrote in *The Scottish Himalayan Expedition,* "Until one is committed, there is hesitancy, the chance to draw back, always ineffectiveness. Concerning all acts of initiative (and creation) there is one elementary truth, the ignorance which kills countless ideas and splendid plans: that the moment one definitely commits oneself, then Providence moves too. All sorts of things occur to help one that would never otherwise have occurred. A whole stream of events issues from the decision, raising in one's favor all manner of unforeseen incidents and meetings and material assistance, which no man could have dreamed would have come his way. I have learned a deep respect for one of Goethe's couplets: 'Whatever you can do, or dream you can, begin it. Boldness has genius, power, and magic in it.'"

The innovator who does that is the innovator who can be king of the world.

!!

References

Books

Altman, Linda J. *Women Inventors,* Facts on File, 1997.

Clarke, Alison J. *Tupperware: The Promise of Plastic in 1950s America,* Smithsonian Institution Press, 1999.

DeLorenzo, Matt. *The New Beetle,* MBI Publishing Company, 1998.

Enrico, Robert. *The Other Guy Blinked: How Pepsi Won the Cola Wars,* Bantam Doubleday Dell, 1988.

Glenmullen, Joseph. *Prozac Backlash,* Simon & Schuster, 2000.

Handler, Ruth. *Dream Doll: The Ruth Handler Story,* Longmeadow Press, 1995.

Kanter, Rosabeth Moss. *Innovation: Breakthrough Thinking at 3M, DuPont, GE, Pfizer, and Rubbermaid,* Harper Business 1997.

Kramer, Peter D. *Listening to Prozac,* Viking, 1993.

Neuharth, Al. *Confessions of an S.O.B.,* Doubleday, 1989.

Sieden, Lloyd S. *Buckminster Fuller's Universe: An Appreciation,* Plenum Press, 1989.

Snyder, Robert. *Buckminster Fuller: An Autobiographical Monologue Scenario,* St. Martin's Press, 1980.

Smith, Douglas K. *Fumbling the Future: How Xerox Invented, Then Ignored, the First Personal Computer,* William Morrow and Company, 1988.

Van Dulken, Stephen. *Inventing the 20th Century,* New York University Press, 2000.

Web Sites

<http://inventors.about.com/science/inventors/
    mbody.htm>
<http://sloan.stanford.edu/mousesite/>
<www.apple.com>
<www.askforfree.com>
<www.atari.com>
<www.bfi.org>
<www.cocacola.com>
<www.crest.com>
<www.dekaresearch.com>
<www.dupont.com>
<www.eisorg.com>
<www.gillette.com>
<www.ideafinder.com/home.htm>
<www.mattel.com>
<www.motorola.com>
<www.mrallbiz.com>
<www.palmpilot.com>
<www.pg.com>
<www.polaroid.com>
<www.prozac.com>
<www.raytheon.com>
<www.sillyputty.com>
<www.tampax.com>
<www.3M.com>
<www.trivialpursuit.com>
<www.tupperware.com>
<www.turfboyusa.com>
<www.usatoday.com>
<www.velcro.com>
<www.viagra.com>
<www.volkswagen.com>
<www.xerox.com>
<www.zenith.com>

!!!!!!!!!!!!!!!!!!!!!!!!!!!!!!!!!!!!!!

Index

The Big Idea

FOR SPECIAL DISCOUNTS on 20 or more copies of *The Big Idea: How Business Innovators Get Great Ideas to Market,* please call Dearborn Trade Special Sales at 800-621-9621, extension 4307.

Dearborn™
Trade Publishing
A **Kaplan Professional** Company